Philip Warner is well known as a military historian and lecturer. He joined the Army after graduating from Cambridge in 1939 and served throughout the war, mainly in the Far East. His books include *Panzer*, *Alamein*, *The D Day Landings*, *The SAS** and *Auchinleck**. Until recently he was a Senior Lecturer at the Royal Military Academy, Sandhurst.

* Also available in Sphere Books

The Special Boat Squadron

PHILIP WARNER

SPHERE BOOKS LIMITED
30–32 Gray's Inn Road, London WC1X 8JL

First published in Great Britain by
Sphere Books Ltd 1983
Copyright © Philip Warner 1983

Set in Times

Printed and bound in Great Britain by
Cox & Wyman Ltd, Reading

Contents

Maps and Diagrams

The Greek Islands	vii
Italy, Sicily and North Africa	vii
The Falklands	viii

Chapter

1	Background to Boatmen	1
2	Early Adventures	8
3	It must get worse before it gets better	23
4	Side by side with the SAS	30
5	Around the Islands	39
6	Keeping up the Pressure	64
7	Widening the Range	79
8	Adriatic Adventures	88
9	Greece	93
10	The Other SBS	112
11	Present Tense	119
12	Cold Water Work	123

Appendices

I	The Cockleshells	130

II	Frogmen and Midget Submarines	133
III	Weapons	136
IV	The Stuka Dive Bomber	138
V	Colonel J. N. Lapraik, DSO, OBE, MC	139
VI	Major T. B. Langton, MC, DL	142
VII	COPPS	145
	Index	146

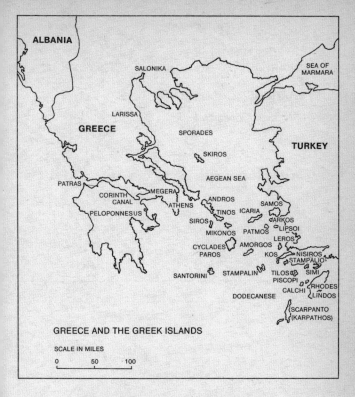

GREECE AND THE GREEK ISLANDS

SCALE IN MILES

0   50   100

MAIN AREAS OF SBS OPERATIONS

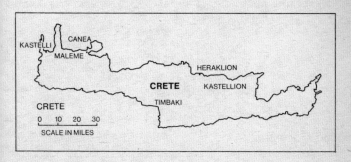

CRETE

0 10 20 30
SCALE IN MILES

MAIN AREAS OF SBS OPERATIONS

SWITZERLAND
AUSTRIA
VENICE
TRIESTE
ISTRA
FIUME
OGULIN
COMMACHIO
CHERSO
OSSERO
LUSSIN
ZARA
GENOA
BOLOGNA
YUGOSLAVIA
ITALY
ADRIATIC SEA
CORSICA
GARGANO
BARI
ROME
NAPLES
TARANTO
AIRFIELD
SARDINIA
Mt ALBERU
TYRRHENIAN SEA
SICILY
CATANIA
AUGUSTA
SYRACUSE
MEDITERRANEAN SEA
MALTA

SICILY, SARDINIA, CORSICA, ITALY
AND THE NORTHERN ADRIATIC
NOTE ISTRIA AND COMMACHIO

0 50 100 150
SCALE IN MILES

NORTH AFRICA
AND ITS
COASTLINE

MEDITERRANEAN SEA
RAS-EL-TIN
BENGHAZI
TOBRUK
ALEXANDRIA
PORT SAID
MATRUH
EL ALAMEIN
CYRENAICA
CAIRO
LIBYA
QATTARA
DEPRESSION
EGYPT
NORTH AFRICA
R. NILE
RED SEA

0 100 200 300
SCALE IN MILES

WEST FALKLAND
SAN CARLOS BAY
EAST FALKLAND
PEBBLE ISLAND
SAN CARLOS
WIRELESS RIDGE
FALKLAND SOUND
FITZROY
PORT STANLEY

THE FALKLAND ISLANDS

0 20 40
SCALE IN MILES

CHAPTER 1

Background to Boatmen

In a Rugby club* bar I used to know there was a saying, 'He's so mobile he could make love standing up in a canoe.' It seemed high praise, suggesting a blend of agility, enthusiasm, and balance. Unfortunately for recruits this it not one of the skills required for admission to the Special Boat Squadron although probably quite a number could qualify. For the SBS always has been, and is, an élite service, demanding high standards of fitness, adaptability and unorthodoxy. In 1983 it is probably the quietest, deadliest, most secret means of reaching a target.

But the boat is always a means to an end, not an end in itself. You can, if you wish, parachute down from the skies carrying a portable boat, and with that boat cross unfordable rivers or traverse immense stretches of water which for all you care can be full of crocodiles. Or you can slip into a canoe from a larger boat and find your way through the reefs, surf, creeks and inlets; you can even transport it over cliffs. You will be able to carry more in your canoe than you can hump on your back, you can turn it over and keep dry under it, you can use it as camouflage. You can be very secret and silent all the time.

The SBS is a young service but the skill it employs is as old as man himself. Back in prehistoric times Man fashioned boats out of tree trunks, and explored rivers, then he made coracles out of twisted osiers (willow); you can still see coracles being used on Welsh rivers today. They seem to float above the water and are, of course, completely portable though too conspicuous for military purposes. The South Sea islanders used canoes to cover enormous distances; other people used Balsa

*The Harlequins. But I am now told that the Welsh club regard canoes as beginners' stuff and say that the real test is a coracle.

rafts; the North American Indians in birch-bark canoes could creep silently up the rivers, come ashore, set a camp ablaze and be a mile or two down river by the time the surviving camp guards came to look for them. Much was learnt from enemies and used against them. In 1869 when the Canadian government bought out the Hudson Bay Company, settlers in the French Red River area rebelled and, led by one Louis Riel, half Indian, half French, murdered a number of British families in the district. The task of restoring law and order was given to Colonel Garnet Wolseley, whose passion for orderly detail gave the Army an expression (now obsolete) 'all Sir Garnet' (i.e. in perfect working order).

Wolseley realized that to conquer Riel's force he would need three battalions (about 3,000 men in all), but to transport that number and capture Riel before he could slip away into the woods and conduct a guerrilla war was a considerable problem. There were no railways or proper roads, only numerous tracks and streams. Wolseley solved the problems by organizing an early Special Boat Squadron, with first-class planning and iron discipline. The troops were instructed on how to travel by land and water. Where the rivers were navigable they embarked in canoes, but when they came to rapids, or places where there were no rivers, they carried their canoes on their backs, a process known as 'portage'. Supplies were kept to essentials and did not include any alcohol. The journey took five weeks only and the soldiers arrived at Riel's headquarters so unexpectedly that he fled from his cabin leaving his breakfast uneaten on the table. With their leader gone (he was captured later after another rebellion), the rebels moved out of the district.

Anyone who has looked at pictures of nineteenth-century soldiers advancing in rigid battle formation, dressed in constricting uniforms, might well wonder how Wolseley transformed such automatons into self-reliant, fast-moving canoeists. But the adaptability of the British soldier is a notable characteristic. In World War II footsloggers became airborne troops and commandos. After World War II, when we were heavily engaged in Malaya and Borneo, it was interesting to discover how soldiers who had been brought up in towns could adapt to becoming stalkers and trappers; some British trackers became better than the local tribesmen who had been practising these skills all their lives. In Malaysia it became clear that there might be no limit to the adaptability of the British serviceman and that the skills learnt in one theatre of operations could easily be used in another. Sheer necessity meant that soldiers had to learn about water, where it was navigable, when drinkable, when lethal (as when contaminated with leptospirosis), when it was manageable swamp and when too treacherous to be trusted. Water can contain the necessities of life such as fish or plants but also enemies of life such as crocodiles, water-snakes (often more deadly than land snakes), and dangerous underwater traps. If you have a portable boat you can travel on water, below which is mud which would suck you down; for a night's rest you can sling it up between two branches, safe from most animals, including man, though not from insects, snakes or leeches. All these skills need to be remembered, otherwise they are forgotten and must be re-learnt, which is laborious and time-consuming.

Rivers can be both an advantage and a disadvantage to a country. On the frontiers they can delay attacks. It is easy to observe what the enemy is planning on the other side of a river and to note where he stands, unless he comes and goes under water or on a very dark night. But even on the darkest night there is usually light on water and any military force consisting of more than a few men is liable to make enough noise to give away their presence.

Rivers can be an enormous liability. Even if you protect the river mouth with booms and chains there are ways of getting under and around them. Often there is a point which is so strong naturally that it is lightly guarded. In 1759 General Wolfe captured Quebec because his army, rowing with muffled oars (padded rowlocks), crept up the St Lawrence river and disembarked on to a virtually unclimbable path, so steep that the French had one sentry only watching it. He heard someone approaching up the path and hastily challenged him; a voice answered, in his own language. As the noise came nearer he realized the climbers were soldiers, so he asked a further question; the answer satisfied him and they came closer. If he had any further suspicions he was never able to voice them, for they killed him very quickly and silently.

Probably the most feared of all sea raiders were the Vikings. Their raids began in the third century A.D., and for many years their ruthlessness and efficiency would daunt the boldest Briton. The Vikings came over the North Sea, calmer then than now, in longboats, using sail when possible and rowing when the wind fell. They were reckless to the point of madness. When the wind blew they crammed on every inch of sail and the harder it blew the more they enjoyed it, even though sometimes their wild ride through the storm ended in a wreck on unexpected rocks or a beach too steep for landing. They could often cover one hundred and fifty miles a day. When they approached the English coast, usually in the dark, they would either row up creeks in their shallow boats, appearing miles inland completely unsuspected; or they would land near a coastal settlement, surround it, massacre the inhabitants, take their horses and raid far inland. They could be raiding Essex one day, Kent the next, Dorset next, leaving a legacy of slaughter, rape, pillage, and burning buildings. Well might people have prayed (as they did): 'From the fury of the Norsemen, Good Lord deliver us.'

Also adding their contribution to the skills of 'special boating' were, of course, the smugglers. For centuries the English Channel was thronged with smugglers, some taking English goods to France, some bringing wine, brandy, tobacco and lace to England. Smugglers were rogues, without a doubt, but very efficient rogues. The English Channel can at times have weather as rough as any sea in the world, hurricanes excepted, as many a modern small boat owner knows to his cost. The darker the night, the rougher the sea, and the more hostile the weather, the better it was for smuggling. With reasonable luck the Excise men would say 'It's too wild for smuggling to-night. We can leave the cutter at her moorings.' Then, like poachers who choose the darkest nights, the smugglers would cross the sea, land on remote beaches, often under cliffs which made them inaccessible except from the sea, and deposit their cargo for distribution later – sometimes they would land, transfer the booty to carts and deliver to customers the same night. To do this successfully, and not finish up at the end of a rope, they had to know the tides, the currents, the coastal paths, the cliffs, the little-used tracks, the probable movements of their enemies the law-enforcers. If you were a successful smuggler you could become a rich and apparently respectable man: if you were unlucky you could be wrecked, drowned, shot in a battle with the Excise men, murdered by your colleagues, or betrayed and hanged. You had to be fit, strong, resourceful, quick-thinking, a good shot, handy with a sword, good at navigation, indifferent to danger and possess a love of adventure for its own sake. You played for high stakes. Your skills would make you a suitable recruit for the SBS but you would be failed on motivation, for smugglers were essentially unpatriotic and self-centred. In the SBS the name of the game is patriotism, and in a tight corner you look after your comrades – if you are lucky enough to have any with you.

The British tradition of seafaring, built up over the centuries in large boats as well as small, includes a considerable history of daring raids. Nelson was a master of changing tactics and was never daunted by being outnumbered and outgunned. Drake is always remembered for his skill in defeating the Spanish Armada in the Channel, using fast manoeuvrable craft and fire ships (in the use of which the British were particularly skilled). But Drake needs to be remembered for more than defeating the Armada or capturing Spanish treasure galleons: Drake saw the sea as a base for long-distance raiding. Britain, strangely enough, has the largest area of coastline in proportion to size of any country in the world. If you have a heavily indented coastline and you rely on fish for your diet, your fishermen acquire skill at finding fresh places to venture. Drake used those probing skills to find new hunting grounds in the seas of the world. The open sea, which could at times be hostile and deadly, was, nevertheless, the entry to all other countries. This attitude to seafaring has influenced other forms of British warfare. In 1941, when Britain's military fortunes were at a very low ebb indeed, a young officer in the Scots Guards conceived the interesting idea that as the Germans had driven the British right back across the desert from Benghazi to near Cairo they might themselves have become highly vulnerable in the process. This idea was greeted with enthusiasm by some, and with considerable scorn by others. The junior officer, whose name was David Stirling, saw the desert as being much akin to the sea (it, had, or course, once been a sea – 50,000 years before), and considered that a vehicle could be just as useful as a boat for raiding. We shall hear more of Stirling later. At this stage he had noted that the Long Range Desert Group – often confused with the SAS but in fact an entirely separate organization – was able to travel for enormous distances in the desert, navigating by a sun compass and the stars. The problem with the desert, as with the sea, is that there are no landmarks, let alone signposts. But the LRDG had developed long range reconnaissance for the purpose of acquiring intelligence. Stirling originally decided to drop by parachute on selected targets along the thinly-stretched German line of communication, hit them hard, walk back into the desert by night, hide under camouflage by day, and then rendezvous with the LRDG. The LRDG, some of whose members later joined the SAS, obligingly agreed to co-operate, although the SAS activities must have alerted the Germans and Italians and therefore made the LRGD task of intelligence gathering more difficult.

After a while, Stirling, who had a nose for a piece of useful equipment, acquired some early Jeeps and equipped them with Vickers K machine-guns taken off Gloster Gladiator aircraft; the guns fired .50 bullets at 1200 rounds a minute. Their style was not unlike raiding with a force of small, fast, heavily-armed gunboats: they arrived at German airfields, delivered their message of several thousand rounds, and departed without waiting for an answer. It was not easy to conceal Jeeps in the desert when the German and Italian aircraft started looking for them, but it was at least easier than it would have been to conceal a flotilla of small boats on the open sea. Strangely enough, pink was the best colour for desert camouflage. As we shall see, the early SBS and the SAS soon became successfully merged, sharing their expertise. The LRDG always remained separate though often co-operating very closely and being involved in many fierce battles. When the desert war came to an end, the LRDG transferred its attention to the Adriatic, where it proceeded to act on those narrow seas in much the same way as it had performed in the sandy expanses of the

Sahara. But long before that happened there were many examples of SAS/SBS joint activities.

It is worth recalling that in pre-war days there were many fewer small boat owners than there are to-day and the moorings on coasts and rivers which the country now possesses did not exist, still less the vast fleet of boats of all types which now fill them. There was, nevertheless, enormous interest in the sea, which was demonstrated by the plentiful supply of recruits for the Royal Navy; the Royal Marines and the Merchant Navy, not to mention the Sea Scouts. And, because plastics were only in their infancy, boats were still made of traditional materials. Boat-building was an art which the British had developed over the years and it had the sort of standards which fit in very well with the SBS. If you build a boat on which your life will at some time depend, you tend to be very careful about design and details. This tradition of boat-building was the origin of that British craftsmanship which made British goods undoubtedly the best and Britain 'the workshop of the world'.

Boats were scarce and often expensive, but boys who want boats will always acquire them somehow or make them. Many boys' magazines described how boats could be built, though some of them were beyond the purse and abilities of the average reader. But in the early 1880s the now defunct *Boy's Own Paper*, a weekly magazine full of stories which made the blood tingle, published an article entitled 'How to make a Canvas Canoe'. The canoe did not, as we might suspect, sink on being lowered into the water; the design was so good and the construction so cheap that the editor was always receiving requests to reprint the article. And it was soon learnt by many a youngster that if you have a light, portable canoe which you have made yourself, you have acquired not merely a boat but a new self-reliance and taste for adventure. Small stones make large ripples.

CHAPTER 2

Early Adventures

The date of the formation of the Special Boat Squadron is a matter of some debate. Officially it is the 14th April 1942, but long before that date SBS forces had been harassing the enemy.

In order to see what opportunities there were for the SBS it is necessary to set the scene. In 1939 Hitler had invaded Poland. Before he could occupy the entire country, his Russian ally Stalin sent in troops to seize the eastern half of Poland. At this point Hitler probably made up his mind that in the near future Russia must be invaded and conquered, but for the moment he left his relationship with his eastern ally as it was and turned his attention to the west. Britain and France, well aware that they had done absolutely nothing to help their ally Poland, now optimistically hoped that Germany had used up all its war materials and would soon be begging for surrender. It was true that Germany was short of certain materials, including steel which was imported from Sweden via Norway, but the remedy for this did not appear to Hitler to be to surrender. Instead, he planned to occupy Norway and isolate Sweden in 'benevolent neutrality', which meant supplying Germany with all her needs without the risk of being bombed.

The moves began on 9th April 1940. Denmark and Norway were invaded, and although Britian despatched a hastily cob-bled-together army to Norway, and although the Navy put in some gallant fighting, the Germans had too much local advantage for them to be ousted. Less than a month later, 10th May, Hitler launched another attack on Holland, Belgium, Luxembourg and eventually France. By mid June all these territories were in German hands. On 1st July the Germans also occupied the Channel Islands; those on Guernsey received a sharp foretaste of what they might be in for when Commandos raided the island on the night of the 14th July, but generally speaking it seemed that Germany now had complete control of the Continent, including Scandinavia. But this was not to be all. On 28th October 1940 Hitler's Italian ally, Mussolini, launched an attack on Greece. Unfortunately for Mussolini, his calculation that forty-five million Italians should be more than a match for seven million Greeks did not prove correct: the latter fought so hard that they drove the Italian invaders right back into Albania and occupied a quarter of that country themselves. Hitler was not pleased at this demonstration of incompetence by his ally, whose troops were being equally unsuccessful in Libya. First he gave support to the Italians in Greece, then as he realized that more than moral and material support was needed, he decided to go in and take the country himself.

The quickest routes from Germany to Greece run through Yugoslavia or Bulgaria. At first the latter route seemed preferable, but in March the Yugoslavs staged a palace revolution that made their 'friendly' co-operation with Germany much less probable. In consequence Hitler decided to tackle Yugoslavia and Greece together, thereby saving his ally and securing part of his own southern flank. In April he launched thirty-three divisions into Yugoslavia and Greece. Yugoslavia was too disorganized and ill-equipped to offer much resistance, and collapsed within ten days. The Germans swept on into Greece, where the going was harder, but by the end of the month they had effectively conquered that country also; they then went on to invade and occupy Crete. With this accomplished, and with Rommel despatched to aid the Italians in the Western Desert, the situation looked particularly good for the Germans. Hitler therefore turned his attention to bigger fish, and on 22nd June 1941 invaded his ally Russia, with over 160 divisions. Huge early successes convinced him – and others – of the correctness of this policy, but the war had been going on for two years only and had another four to run.

One bonus of the occupation of Greece was the possession of the Greek islands which are scattered from the northern Aegean to the Cyclades; Germany also controlled the Adriatic coastline up to Trieste. The northern group of islands in the Aegean are known as the Sporades, and the eastern as the Dodecanese. Strictly speaking the Dodecanese consist of Nisyros, Cos, Palmos, Kasos, Leros, Tilos, Calchi, Simi, Stampalia, Lipsos, Scarpanto and Kalymnos but Rhodes and Castelrosso are usually included with them: many of these names will figure strongly in the pages which follow.

For Britain the outlook in late 1941 could not have been bleaker. All her principal allies had been conquered and overrun, formerly friendly neutrals had either been overrun or put in a German stranglehold which made them unable to help Britain further; supplies lost to Britain had now become available to the enemy; since 1939 Britain and her allies had experienced nothing but a long run of defeats from an apparently invincible enemy. And worse was to come. The U-boat campaign was scoring heavy successes in the Atlantic, bombs were now falling on British cities, and by the beginning of the following year – although Britain could not in her wildest dreams have imagined it – her cherished Far Eastern possessions, with their invaluable rubber and tin – would have fallen into the hands of another ruthless enemy, Japan. Apart from Spain and Portugal there was not an inch of coastline from Scandinavia to the eastern Mediterranean which the Germans did not control, for even if they had no troops on the spot there was constant surveillance by aircraft or coastal craft. German power looked absolutely secure – or everywhere vulnerable – it all depended on the way you viewed these matters. To a number of optimists, many of whom found their way into the SBS, it looked vulnerable. The problem was where to start, what with, and with what specific objective. Isolated raids can be expensive and pointless; raiding, to be effective, must be coordinated and related to the war effort.

The importance of raiding had already occurred to the Higher Command. It is interesting to note how many effective anti-German measures were begun even when Britain was reeling with shock from one defeat after another in mid 1940. While the rest of the world was waiting for Britain to give up the unequal struggle and surrender, Britain was planning airborne and sea raids, radar development, flame projectiles, new weapons, even the organization for rehabilitating other countries when they had all been liberated.

The problem of where to start was said to have been solved by Lt Wilson and Marine Hughes; they landed in Italy from a submarine and canoe on 22nd Jan 1941 and blew up a railway tunnel and the train passing through it.

The reason why 'hit and run' raiding had occurred to the Higher Command was that Admiral Sir Roger Keyes had firmly implanted it in their minds. He was respected throughout the Navy as the man who planned and led the Zeebrugge Raid on 23rd April 1918. The 'raid' consisted of a surprise attack to destroy the base and block the canal which the Germans were using to great effect against Allied North Sea and Channel shipping. It was a suicidal mission if ever there was one, but by speed and daring it succeeded in its aims without too depressing a casualty list.

In the first seven months of World War II there was no action except that of the Germans and Russians in Poland, U-boat attacks on our shipping, and leaflet dropping raids over Germany. Chamberlain was Prime Minister; Churchill was First Lord of the Admiralty. Then came the Blitzkrieg. Chamberlain resigned, and Churchill became Prime Minister – not a moment too soon, for the Germans were now at the coasts of Western Europe from the Arctic Circle to the Eastern Mediterranean. Even as the British were dismally evacuating Dunkirk, Churchill, Keyes and another intrepid and ingenious warrior, Lt Col Dudley Clarke, were planning to hit back. The first Commando raid took place on the night of 23rd June, less than three weeks after Dunkirk; it was proposed to enter and damage Boulogne harbour, but surprise had been lost and the pioneer Commandos re-embarked to use their experience in planning further raids, one of which, as we saw above, was to be on Guernsey soon afterwards.

Intensive training of Commandos and others now took place in rugged areas of Scotland, such as Lochailort and around the Isle of Arran. There Commandos and others were taught how to survive in hostile conditions, kill silently and swiftly, use explosives, find their way around in uncharted territory, land on unfriendly beaches, negotiate barbed wire and practise various other unsocial skills. As may be guessed, the personalities who were attracted to instructing and being instructed in these esoteric arts were often people with world-wide experience in unusual adventures. Among them was one Roger Courtney who had spent his life canoeing, big-game hunting and generally avoiding being in any place which was safe or comfortable. Courtney had a scorn for people who prided themselves on their simple toughness. What he required, and got, was people whose toughness was exceeded by their quick-thinking and intelligence. His detachment, which was to do the preliminary reconnaissance for Commando raids, was called the 'Folboat Section', folboats being folding or otherwise collapsible boats. At this stage Courtney had as his second-in-command Lt Wilson of the Royal Artillery; Wilson was later to pioneer the first SBS operation in conjunction with Marine Hughes. The long-term objective of the Folboat training was to assist a raid by No 8 Commando on Pantellaria, a small island lying between Sicily and Italy. The proposed invasion never took place, and much later some heavy bombing by the RAF forced the 11,000 Italians on the island to surrender without further fighting. This would appear to have been fortunate, for the possibilities of one Commando of less than a thousand men, preceded by a dozen or so SBS, overcoming 11,000 securely-based and well-armed enemy soldiers might appear rather optimistic: whatever the result there would have been plenty of people killed, on both sides. The next possibility was an attack on Rhodes, for which 7th, 8th and 11th Commandos were earmarked. This mixed unit was called 'Layforce' from the name of its commander, Colonel Robert Laycock. But, remarkable though it may seem, Folboats were still scarcely recognized as having a permanent existence. Not least of the reasons was the fact that if any of the folboats which went out with Layforce were damaged – and undoubtedly they would be – they could not be repaired or replaced in the Middle East.

The attack on Rhodes was then cancelled as every available boat was needed for the evacuation of British forces from Greece. In the closing stages of the German conquest of Greece the small British force which had been – unwisely – sent

12

from the desert to assist the Greeks rather than to win Wavell's next battle in North Africa, endeavoured to get out of the country and save soldiers even if valuable equipment was lost. This particular predicament was due to Churchill overriding Wavell and bolstering weakness rather than reinforcing strength: it is a good military principle to reinforce strength and to gain victories from which other victories can proceed later.

Apparently there was now nothing left for Folboats, which had been built up to a total of thirty-eight, (eight officers and thirty soldiers). As with most 'special forces', the distinction between officers and men was narrower than in more formal units: interdependence was the keynote, as was mutual respect. There were no problems with discipline: everyone knew where he stood, what he could do, and what others could do better. Their uniform was what might be described as 'working dress'; they had no special badges or distinctive markings. They were a fringe unit, liable to be disbanded at any time, their personnel dispersed to other units, their carefully developed skills lost. Fortunately at this stage Courtney, sensing the danger which threatened, arranged for Folboats to be transferred to HMS *Medway*, a mother ship for the submarine flotilla. Here they could practise their skills working with submarines. It seemed almost too good to be true. He found an ally in Admiral Maund, Director of Combined Operations at GHQ in Cairo. Maund saw no reason why submarines should not be able to find room for one or two men with a folding canoe or inflatable boat who wished to harry the enemy coastal forces. It would be good training for everyone, and could upset enemy morale: enemy morale badly needed upsetting at that moment.

The first raid, small though it was, had been so successful that a repeat performance was clearly necessary. Once again Wilson and Hughes were given the go-ahead. This time they embarked on the submarine *Utmost*, carrying approximately 500 lbs of explosives. When one considers how much damage can be done with one or two pounds of explosive, it will be realized that 500 lbs would make a very sizeable impression. Once more the west coast of Italy offered the most suitable target; a railway tunnel seemed as good an objective as any. But the attempt to do even more damage than previously made this expedition laborious: one doesn't carry 500 lbs of explosives between two men over rocky beaches in unknown country without some difficulty. Several trips had to be made from the canoes to the destined tunnel. Unfortunately, just after the charges had been laid a party of Italian soldiers came through the tunnel and spotted them. Wilson decided to attack; they retreated hastily and aroused the nearby village. Frustrated, Wilson and Hughes moved back to the beach, re-embarked, and found a secure, sheltered cove for the night. The next evening they tried their luck in Sicily, where they found a three-span railway bridge over the River Oliva. Alas, this too was well guarded; there was a brief exchange of fire before Wilson and Hughes decided that all hope of surprise had now vanished and they must try again another day elsewhere.

Other excursions were taking place with the aid of other submarines. Courtney landed at Scutari in Albania – it is now called Shkoder. Here he observed that the Italian guards were actively preparing for attack by making fortifications; this at least was encouraging. Lt James Sherwood and Cpl Booth then undertook the task of escorting eight Special Operations Executive personnel to Crete to work with the Cretan partisans. Sherwood and Booth carefully ferried their cargo ashore, instructing those who had already landed to await the arrival of the others before exercising any initiative and doing any personal exploring. By the time Sherwood and Booth got the final party ashore the earlier arrivals had vanished, deciding to ignore the instructions of the ferrymen. Instead, four belligerent-looking Cretans appeared; these were partisans, and a brisk battle was narrowly avoided. The SBS began to realize that it is easier to arrive unobtrusively in a heavily populated area than it is in a remote district where the local people know the countryside like the back of their hands and have an instinct for discovering what is going on in it.

Wilson now decided that a trip further afield might be more productive. He hitched a lift on the submarine *Truant* which was examining the Adriatic, and landed close to Ancona on 26th October 1941 conveniently close to the Brindisi-Milan railway line. They moved in swiftly and laid their charges on the line. By the time the explosion took place Wilson and

Hughes were already boarding the submarine, but were able to observe the devastation. The damage was enormous; they had not only wrecked the track but also a long troop train with it.

By this time the special skills of Folboats were being constantly used to ferry in SOE personnel who were planning to link up with potential resistance groups. Most of the SOE personnel whom Folboats encountered had little objection to living in hostile territory where they would be tortured and shot if discovered, but complained that the trip in the submarine made them queasy and the journey by canoe and over the beach was a complete nightmare – everyone to his taste!

Suddenly a larger operation loomed: this one was the brainchild of Keyes' own son. The plan was to land in Libya and capture or kill Rommel. In spite of postwar attempts to undervalue Rommel, there is no doubt that he was the inspiration of the German and Italian forces in the desert and his removal, one way or the other, would have made a very considerable difference to the Allied efforts in that theatre.

The raiding party was much too large, numbering fifty-nine in all; it was drawn from Layforce and the appointed night was 17th November 1941. Two submarines were assigned, and the party landed on the beach in rubber boats. The expedition seemed to be dogged by ill luck from the start. Bad weather made the landing extremely difficult, and once ashore the party found that rough terrain and continuing adverse weather made progress erratic, slow and unpleasant. But they were on land, and the two submarines, *Torbay* and *Talisman*, would not return to pick them up for another four days. Much was likely to happen to them before that moment arrived.

The journey inland to their target took so long that they were beginning to doubt the honesty, as well of the knowledge, of the Arab guides when finally they arrived at their destination. But Rommel was not in the area, let alone in that house: he was on a quick visit to Rome.

This was an early raid and a number of mistakes were made; later, the SAS and SBS both used this raid in training as an example of how *not* to make a raid. In that aspect the Rommel expedition proved useful and doubtless saved many lives later, but one of its casualties was the leader, Lt Col Geoffrey Keyes, who was awarded a posthumous VC. There are two accounts of the sequence of events, one the British, the other the German. The British version is that the party went through the building, opening doors and throwing in grenades where they found occupants; in one room the occupants were sufficiently alert to shoot when the door opened, and this was when Keyes was killed.

The German version is that a sentry inside the building was suspicious of the intruders and grappled with them in the dark. This raised the alarm and the orderly officer ran downstairs nd shot at the first man he saw, who happened to be Keyes. The house was not one ever used by Rommel, but the HQ of Supply Services; it was thus well protected and full of soldiers. Once the alarm was raised and there was no trace of Rommel, the raid was abandoned. Although the party had begun fifty-nine strong, a group of that size would have been easily disposed of once the Germans concentrated troops on the area. As it was several of the Commando were killed and others were wounded or captured; the remainder made their way back to the beach. Those captured should – according to Hitler's strict orders – have been shot, for that was to be the fate of Commandos and other raiders, but Rommel disregarded the order. He did not shoot prisoners, even if they were men who had come with the specific task of killing him. There was a marked contrast between Rommel and the thugs who comman- ded the Waffen SS.

The return to the beach was full of incident. Twenty-two out of the original fifty-nine struggled back; no one had any idea of the fate of the remainder – some had escaped inland but most had been captured. Unfortunately the boats in which they had landed and which they thought they had effectively concealed had now disappeared. An attempt was made to reach them by rubber boats from the submarine, but this failed because the rough sea snatched the buoyant boat away from the side of the submarine before anyone could get into it. There were no other boats which could be used to rescue the party and it was suggested rather optimistically that they might like to swim for it. The suggestion was not well received: the chances of survival, let alone of reaching the submarine, seemed minimal.

All this was of course being contemplated in the dark. As dawn approached the submarine had to leave and conceal itself unless it wished to become a target for aircraft, depth-charges, shore-based guns and other unfriendly devices. Before departing it signalled its intention of returning the next night. This was not a particularly wise thing to do, as others than the commandos could have understood the message. When the submarine returned the following night, there were no signals from the beach. It was therefore decided that yet another SBS reconnaissance should be attempted. This time the recce party consisted of Lt T. B. Langton and Cpl Feebery. Langton, who had arrived in the SBS from the Irish Guards, was a Cambridge rowing blue of considerable repute but, like most university oarsmen, was distinctly on the large side, nearly fourteen stone. His partner was no smaller, so although they were ideal for moving the flimsy boat they contributed rather less to its stability in the lively surf. They landed and walked to where they had seen a light, even though it was not giving the correct signal. There seemed to be a suspicious amount of activity in the area, and no English words to be heard, so the pair returned to the boat and re-embarked. Somewhat recklessly they edged along the outside of the surf, looking for survivors of Keyes' party. There was no one to be seen, not even a German. They returned to the submarine and as dawn broke examined the beach again through the periscope. It was now covered with enemy soldiers, who were clearly preparing a welcome for any landing party from the submarine. They must have observed Langton and Feebery with astonishment, but refrained from firing on them in the hope that the canoeists would report the beach as safe and make some rash move which might compromise the submarine; if so, their ruse was doomed to failure.

So far the SBS had had an almost unofficial existence; soon it was to be put on a more formal footing. Today, many years after the final curtain has dropped on World War II, it is a mystery to many people, particularly those in the regular forces, how the war managed to foster so many small, unorthodox formations like the SBS. Wherever one looks there was private enterprise and even 'private armies'; there was a constant stream of agents and spies, some landed in enemy territory by the SBS, some parachuted in, and others gently infiltrated through neutral countries. Portugal, Spain, Sweden and Switzerland were all neutral; it used to be said there were more foreign agents in Lisbon than Portuguese citizens.

Spies in general were organized by Special Operations Executive which trained, supplied, gave instructions and co-ordinated. Private armies tend to be a law unto themselves, which may be one reason why they acquired the nickname 'the funnies'. The 'private enterprise' type of force came into existence because for much of the War there were considerable numbers of soldiers (and sailors) who had been trained but for whom no immediate use could be found. After Dunkirk there was no large-scale military activity launched from England until the Normandy invasion of 1944. Soldiers were, of course, sent to the Middle East and Far East, but a substantial number were retained in Britain for the invasion. All that could be done with them was to train them, employ them in exercises, and re-train them. Spread over three years this becomes rather tedious and there was therefore no lack of volunteers for any enterprise, however hazardous, which offered a change of scene and occupation. Some tried for the Commandos, others for parachuting, others volunteered to be spies. One of the most enterprising of the unorthodox formations was Phantom, which set itself the task of finding out exactly what was happening in the front line and passing this information directly to headquarters and places where it could best be used.

The feeling of stalemate was no less marked in the Middle East. Once we had lost Greece and Crete there was little for soldiers to do except engage in the desert battles, most of which seemed to be specially suitable for tanks only. There were a number of infantrymen who had volunteered for Commando raiding while in England and who now found themselves unable to do much because of shortage of shipping. Out of these resources – a number of fit, enterprising soldiers who had volunteered for Commando work but were not now going to be able to practise it – David Stirling created the Special Air Service. Such enterprises were not discouraged officially, for it was felt that they kept men actively employed; they were less

18

popular with commanding officers who were often infuriated by losing some of their best men to what they felt were merely crackpot enterprises.

But the SBS had done enough to justify its continued existence. In December 1941 Courtney was posted back to Scotland where he was given the authority to train a small section for special boat work. It was to be the Special Boat Section of the Special Service Brigade. Much of its training was to take place in the less hospitable areas of the north. There they learned to handle boats in rough seas on dangerous coasts, to move from sea to land and back carrying various forms of weapons, to cross harbour and river booms, and to lay and lift mines. They also had to become proficient at signalling. This section did much to develop methods of cliff climbing and descending. Navigation on sea and land was given a high priority; few people are more useless than enthusiasts who do not know where they are, still less where they ought to be.

The SBS, as constituted on 14th April 1942, consisted of forty-seven men, including all ranks. It was commanded by (now) Major R. J. Courtney, MC, and the second-in-command was Captain G. C. S. Montanaro from the Royal Engineers. Montanaro knew more about explosives than most people.

Courtney was succeeded in the Middle East by Captain M. Kealy. This part of the SBS had learnt more from experience than from training and had attracted a number of formidable warriors. Among them was a young lieutenant from the Black Watch, David Sutherland, 'a man who only spoke if he had something to say', and Eric Newby, later to become famous as an author (*A Traveller's Life* and *Love and War in the Apennines*). Another writer was John Lodwick, a fluent French speaker; Lodwick was a colourful personality, and very talented. He was killed in a car crash in Spain in 1959.

The departure of Courtney, although regretted, had not slowed down the activities of the Middle East SBS. In December 1941 the old team of Wilson and Hughes tried their luck in Navarino (now Pylos) harbour. They were transported appropriately near by the submarine *Torbay*, which was used to this sort of activity. They were looking for suitable ships to damage but were observed and fired on before they could come close enough to find targets. After leaving an interval for the panic to subside, they tried again. The rumour that there were enemy destroyers in the harbour proved to be correct; one was lying off the end of the pier. Wilson proposed to attach a limpet charge and swam quietly towards the destroyer. Unfortunately the weather was bitterly cold and the water more so; this was before the days of elaborate protective clothing. By the time he reached the destroyer he was too numb to handle his lethal charge. As he fumbled around, Hughes, disturbed at the length of time this was taking and fearing for Wilson's safety, gave a tug on the line and then began to haul him back. At any other time of year the venture might have succeeded, but not in December. They had learnt something from the experience. Nowadays we know much more about the hazards of exposure to cold and wet; often they can be overcome, but not always. Modern protective clothing can stave off the worst effects, but not invariably, nor necessarily over a very long period. In the early days of the SBS it was all a matter of trial and error.

One of the more interesting trials was when David Stirling enlisted the help of the SBS to assist him in damaging shipping at Buerat harbour in Tripoli. The SAS plan was to destroy trucks, fuel dumps, the wireless station *and* ships. Ships were a problem as they were anchored off shore. However, one canoe would suffice to do the rounds while the German and Italian attention was diverted elsewhere. Accordingly a folboat (Captain Duncan, Cpl Barr) was allocated and loaded on to a thirty cwt truck. The experience proved harsher for the folboat than the roughest seas might have been: when it was unloaded it was no longer seaworthy. The SBS men, not wishing to waste their time, then joined in the land-based operation and used their explosives to add to the general wave of destruction. This period also saw an amazing rescue in which Langton spent five hours in the water holding the semi-conscious Sherwood after a folboat had capsized.*

Another SBS 'first' was now scored by Corporal Booth. So close was the liaison between the submarine crew and the SBS that the latter were now allowed to become machine-gunners in

* See Appendix VI

20

surface battles. On one such occasion the submarine *Torbay* came to the surface to capture a supply ship. Unhappily for the sub the supply ship opened up with a heavy calibre gun as they came into range. This was enough for Booth. He swivelled his Bren towards the enemy gun, killed the crew in one burst, turned it on to another party manning a gun and then on to the bridge. Not surprisingly he received a Distinguished Conduct Medal.

The SBS had now become so well-known and versatile that it was inevitable that GHQ would find more tasks for it, even though these bordered on the suicidal or the impossible. It is the experience of unorthodox units that after beginning in the face of scorn, frustration, and official disapproval, they are then honoured in everything except rank, promotion, pay, equipment and decorations, and are expected to take on the most absurd and fanciful tasks. Requests for a larger establishment and more generous supplies meet with a less enthusiastic reception.

On this occasion some enlightened thinker in GHQ had decided that the SBS was the ideal means to conduct unobtrusive reconnaissance. For some reason which was never clearly explained, GHQ Cairo wished to know more about German activities along the coastline west of Gazala. Glad to be of service to the mandarins who might control their further employment and existence, the SBS produced Captain K. Allot and Lt. D. Ritchie, RN to perform the arduous task. They set off in a Motor Torpedo Boat from Tobruk on 22nd May 1942 and travelled with it to Cape Ras-el-Tin. There they went ashore and began their reconnaissance. First they lay up and watched. Nothing happened and it seemed all rather uneventful.

Then Germans started arriving, and the astonished SBS counted two hundred men. The German troopers proceeded to disport themselves actively, first with PT then with that game which civilians call 'hide and seek' and the services call 'E and E' (Escape and Evasion): fortunately the one place no one chose to hide or to seek in was the SBS hiding place. By the time Allot and Ritchie had watched these games all day long, they decided they would be justified in reporting a German presence in the area, particularly on the coast. On this occasion – it was the first time ever – they had a radio and sent a message to report mission accomplished and that they were returning. The fact that they were about 150 miles from base, separated from it by a stretch of unknown enemy-held coastline with attendant patrol boats, and that they would need to do most of their travelling by night, often in rough water, were details they tried to ignore. But they made it, all 150 miles of it. It was a record of sorts, for although people have subsequently travelled longer distances in similar craft they have not had to contend with quite such exacting circumstances. Allot had been at school at Radley, which is famed for rowing – but had not been a rowing enthusiast.

CHAPTER 3

It must get worse before its gets better

The situation in the Middle East by mid 1942 had considerable bearing on the future employment of the SBS.

Britain was in considerable difficulties after the lost battles of 1940; to Mussolini this seemed an ideal moment to extend his holdings in Africa and therefore impress Hitler, his ally in what was known as the Rome/Berlin Axis. The Italians were already in Ethiopia as a result of a short, murderous, and unprovoked war they had conducted there in 1935. On 5th August 1940 Italian troops had entered British Somaliland. As the Italians had 350,000 troops available in Ethiopia and Britain had only 1500 in Somaliland it was decided that the Italian army could have the country for the time being. Much encouraged, the Italians then decided to invade Egypt from Libya where they had another 250,000 men under the command of Marshal Balbo. That was in September 1940 and although the British forces in Egypt numbered only 30,000 they were used so adroitly that Balbo called off the offensive, contentedly settled down on the frontier, and signalled to Italy for more reinforcements. Wavell and O'Connor then decided that enough was enough and proceeded to roll back the Italians in both areas, taking prisoners in enormous numbers. Properly led and motivated the Italians could be an effective fighting force, so just when Italian fortunes reached their lowest ebb in February 1941 Hitler despatched a contingent of German troops to Libya to remedy the deficiencies. Soon they were joined by Erwin Rommel, a German tank commander who had handled a German armoured division with considerable dash and initiative in the battle for France. With the arrival of Rommel and some first-class equipment, including 88 millimetre guns and Panzer IV tanks, the desert battles now became a very different story. Not least of the British difficulties was the fact that they possessed no gun capable of penetrating the German tank armour except the 25-pdr, and the 25-pdr was not the sort of gun which could be fitted to a tank. There followed a series of battles which ranged from Benghazi in the west to El Alamein in the east. The area of conflict was approximately 1200 miles long and extended hundreds of miles to the south. It was ideal for wide, sweeping, encircling movements, if you had the fuel; it was equally an area in which you could become hopelessly lost even without the aid of one of the frequent sandstorms which could blow up from nowhere and completely change yesterday's landscape.

The conflict which ranged back and forth over this area became known to troops – who have the aptitude for the right nicknames – as the 'Benghazi handicap'. You were either rushing forward capturing all before you, or retreating after some disaster, hoping not to get cut off before you reached 'the wire', as the Libyan/Egyptian frontier came to be called. In November 1941 Britain had begun a victorious sweep to clear the Germans out of North Africa but it had gone wrong, Rommel had adroitly counter-attacked and there was stale-mate from January onwards. But in May, just when Britain was about to renew her onslaught on the German positions, Rommel attacked first. Auchinleck, who was commanding the British forces, would have been more than a match for Rommel if the standard of tank and gun had been even roughly equivalent. But the British armour was sadly deficient. This time it seemed as if Rommel really would reach Cairo, but Auchinleck stopped him in the Alamein position in July. Soon afterwards Auchinleck was dismissed, quite unjustly, by Chur-chill in one of the latter's more impetuous moments, and Montgomery replaced him. Not long after Mongomery's arri-val there followed supplies of Sherman tanks which were a match for the Germans, and 17-pdr guns which could penetrate the armour plate on the German tanks – but in mid 1942 with Auchinleck still grimly holding the Alamein position, the future looked anything but radiant. To complete this somewhat dark picture it is worth recalling that the Germans were now firmly and apparently immovably established in Russia, and that the Japanese controlled the Far East from India to Hawaii and from Korea to New Guinea.

The next German move, *if* they reached Cairo, would be to link up their armies by a thrust down through Syria. This move would have appealed to Hitler; it also appealed to the SBS. Syria, they felt, was a place where the Germans could be hit really hard. The SBS were perhaps more aware of the events of military history than Hitler was. In previous centuries, conquering heroes from Alexander the Great to Napoleon had usually gone just that bit too far. Finally, with their lines over-extended, with their troops exhausted or without motivation for anything but enjoying their booty, the tide turned; the guerrillas, the resistance groups, got to work and the great conquest began to sag and crumble. That was the way Stirling, Sutherland, Langton, Courtney and others saw the future in World War II – even in the darkest hour.

So the SBS made a reconnaissance of Syria. Not only did they examine it for all suitable creeks, inlets, and ambush points, they also surveyed it for caves which could be used as secret hiding places and ammunition dumps. A guerrilla force which begins its activities with an insufficient supply of ammunition, hoping to capture more from the enemy, is unlikely to continue its existence for long. There are many ways in which guerrillas can disturb an army of occupation but very few indeed can be managed without adequate supplies of ammunition and explosives.*

The SBS was now finding that it was drawing closer and closer to the SAS, partly because of an identity of aim and partly through sharing personnel and supplies. It was therefore logical that the efforts of the two units should be co-ordinated and that if the SBS was raiding a harbour the SAS should be attending to a nearby airfield. Stirling, whose creative thinking never stopped for one moment, had already formed a unit which could operate from the sea. This had been put under the command of Captain the Earl Jellicoe. Jellicoe was the son of Admiral of the Fleet, Earl Jellicoe, who had been the guiding spirit of the Royal Navy during World War I. He commanded

---

*Their reconnaisance, which lasted some three months, also reported on the feasibility of a defensive line.

the Fleet at the Battle of Jutland in 1916 and as a result of his efforts on that occasion the German Navy never challenged the British Fleet again during the war. The son had not followed the father into the Navy but had proceeded from Winchester to Trinity College, Cambridge (the same college as David Stirling) and at the outbreak of World War II had joined the Coldstream Guards. After the events narrated in these pages, for which he received the DSO and MC, he joined the Foreign Office and later went into politics. He held many ministerial posts, including that of 1st Lord of the Admiralty.

In June the SBS were pleased to be given permission to land on Crete and destroy what they could find on its three airfields, Heraklion, Kastelli and Timbaki. This operation had to be co-ordinated with the SAS, principally for the reason that the latter appeared to have an unlimited, almost magical supply of explosives and other lethal devices. Stirling decided to synchronize this with an attack the SAS was making on six airfields in Cyrenaica, but also wished for SAS involvement in the raid on Crete, if only for the experience.

Accordingly Jellicoe was allotted Heraklion with an SAS group, and the SBS were to concentrate on the others – Kastelli and Timbaki, with Maleme added to compensate for the loss of Heraklion. The Kastelli raid went exceptionally well, destroying a variety of enemy valuables, including six aircraft; Timbaki (allocated to Sutherland and Riley) proved a disappointment in that it was abandoned and deserted; and at Maleme any attempt at sabotage was clearly impossible for the airfield was defended and garrisoned like a fortress. As the Maleme party was made up of Kealey, Allot and Feebery, it will be realized that if such seasoned campaigners thought an attack was impossible it was impossible. Their only consolation prize was to take off eight New Zealanders who had escaped capture at the battle for Crete and were only too glad to exchange mere survival for a more active rôle.

Jellicoe's raid, although not strictly SBS, was so closely akin to it that it requires a mention here, and Jellicoe later commanded a squadron of the SBS. The Heraklion raid involved a larger party than usual. As well as Jellicoe it included a Greek guide named Lt Costi and four Frenchmen, one being Com-

26

mandant Bergé. The Frenchmen were there for the experience; it was unlikely that there would be much call for French interpreters on Crete. They travelled by submarine (*Triton*) and rubber boat. Their attempts to pass themselves off as Germans fell rather flat when the Cretans addressed them in English; this may have been because there were still many survivors of the Crete battle wandering around on the island. Their journey towards Heraklion was slower than had been anticipated. Those who know Crete – and many nowadays do – will have observed that it is rugged and difficult country if you avoid the roads, which Jellicoe's party was bound to do. When they finally approached the outskirts of Heraklion they found that German servicemen were more numerous than they had been given reason to expect. The field was also surrounded by barbed wire. By this time the party was feeling the effects of several days at sea, clambering over mountains, lack of nourishing food, lack of sleep, and exposure to some very cold nights. It might seem surprising that the weather in Crete in June could be testing, but up in the hills it certainly was. Several times they nearly ran into German patrols.

Nevertheless they cut a hole in the wire round the airfield, slipped through it and hid in a supply dump. Almost immediately the hole in the wire was discovered. Fortunately for the intruders an RAF aircraft came over and dropped a series of bombs. None hit the airstrip but their arrival was so unexpected – the RAF pilot had followed some German aircraft in, unnoticed until he dropped his bombs – that it caused a diversion in which the hole in the wire was forgotten and Jellicoe and his friends were able to move around unnoticed in the general confusion. There were over sixty planes on the airfield but they only had time to attend to sixteen; all of them were in allegedly bomb-proof shelters.

The technique of blowing up enemy aircraft had been developed some months before by David Stirling and 'Jock' Lewes. When the SAS was being formed finding the most effective weapons was a major problem. How much explosive was needed to do irreversible damage to an aeroplane? The minimum quantity must be used because everything, detonators included, had to be carried. A man carrying an awkward, heavy load is not likely to move quickly or quietly.

Lewes experimented with time-pencils so that delayed action bombs could be laid on aircraft and left to go off later. To travel hundreds of miles to blow up a single aircraft was a waste of time. However, to lay charges on about fifty planes, creeping up unobserved and if necessary dealing swiftly and silently with anyone guarding them, was obviously going to take time; and the charges must go off simultaneously *after* the raiders had got away.

A time-pencil was a device containing acid which when set would eat through the seal to the detonator; the detonator would set off its big brother, the heavy explosive charge. The specification and manufacture of the time-pencils had to be absolutely right.

Although Lewes was never in the SBS he did Commando sea-raiding around Tobruk; he was killed early on in the SAS by an Italian aircraft when returning from a raid. Not everyone has the temperament to experiment with explosives but Lewes had, which was fortunate for the SBS and SAS. Lewes was an Australian from King's School, Paramatta who had gone on to Oxford. At his college (Christ Church) he had quickly made his mark as an oarsman, won a blue, and become President of the Oxford boat. At this time Oxford had sustained a series of thirteen consecutive defeats by Cambridge and it was being suggested that Oxford would never be able to win the Boat Race again because the river at Oxford was inadequate for practice, that Oxford no longer attracted the best oarsmen, and so on. Lewes was undeterred by these gloom and doom speakers and trained a crew which ended Cambridge's run of victories. At the last minute he decided he was not good enough to row in it himself, so he dropped himself. A quieter and more unassuming personality would be difficult to find. When war was declared he joined the Welsh Guards and soon volunteered for the Commandos. This brought him into Layforce and the SAS.

The first charges had been laid on Heraklion airfield to go off after an hour and a half; subsequent ones obviously had a shorter existence. The party just had time to distribute a few more explosives on lorries and petrol dumps before they noticed that a party of Germans was leaving the airfield, presumably for patrol work. Jellicoe, guessing that the patrol had been made up from different units and that its members would not necessarily know each other, decided to join on behind. The ruse was successful. As they left, their delayed action charges started to explode all over the airfield.

In order to avoid detection they split up into very small groups. The French were betrayed by Cretan peasants and captured, but Jellicoe and Costi, having walked 120 miles over the roughest of tracks, were taken off by a lurking caïque. A caïque is a small trading schooner much favoured in Greek and Turkish waters. The seas abound with them, and the fact that one was skippered by a Royal Navy lieutenant, not in uniform, passed unnoticed by the Germans.

So far there had been a record of successes, hard won, but won none the less. Duncan was briefed to destroy targets in Sicily and to assist him he had such tried stalwarts as Newby, Booth, Duffy and Dunbar. Alas, the entire group was captured by Germans on the night they landed in Sicily before they could even begin to make themselves unwelcome guests. Another blow was the capture of Wilson – a founder member and the most experienced in all – in Tobruk harbour where he was looking for ships on which to put charges. Sherwood, Barnes, Alexander and Gurney landed on the coast a few miles to the west of Alamein and set about destroying a large German supply dump. To reach their objective they had to walk through German camp lines, threading their way past tents and barracks. The mission was successful, but once the alarm was raised getting away was impossible. The Germans were quick to learn. The numbers in the SBS were now becoming very low indeed.

There was only one solution. Their work was very similar to and often co-ordinated with that of the SAS, and it was logical that they should become even more closely allied by using SAS personnel, who were nothing if not adaptable.

CHAPTER 4

Side by Side with the SAS

Reinforced from their new comrades-in-arms, the SBS set to work on new tasks. A useful addition to their ranks was a small Greek contingent, for the Greek Sacred Squadron had also allied itself to the SAS. The Greek Sacred Squadron had a tradition of refusing no task and dying to the last man, if necessary. A party consisting of Sutherland, Allot, Moss, McKenzie, Duggan, Barrow and three Greeks formed up in the Lebanon and made preparations for one of the biggest operations yet – a raid on Rhodes. There were two large and important airfields on Rhodes – Marizza and Calato, and the Germans were using their facilities extensively for harassing British shipping in the Mediterranean.

The SBS set off in a Greek submarine *Papanikolis* for a four-day voyage. The problem with all these trips was that those unused to the air and conditions in submarines usually found both so upsetting that they began the next stage in anything but the best of health. On the other hand, submariners separated from the smell of oil and stale air and put in a healthy, breezy place would be down with a cold in no time.

When transferred to shore the raiders had the onerous task of finding their way over treacherously rugged countryside in the dark; even a sprained ankle can immobilize a man in such conditions. Unfortunately the guides were not used to these out-of-the-way routes and they soon confessed to being lost, but the party managed to reach a point some five miles inland without losses of anything but time. They then divided: Sutherland headed for Calato and Allot for Marizza. Sutherland reached the airfield after an unpleasant and rainy journey. For the immediate attack his party was divided again: Calambikidis, Barrow and Harris in one section, and Sutherland and

Duggan (a Marine) in the other. The aim of this was that the two groups should approach the airfield from opposite sides, and if one was forestalled the other might get through. It worked well in the early stages. Sutherland found a number of unguarded aircraft and dumps, and left bombs on them. Then he returned to a point outside the airfield from which he could observe results. He did not have to wait long. There was also evidence that the other section had been both active and successful. But a more ominous sound came an hour later: the sound of exchange of fire from rifles and automatics. Clearly the other party had run into trouble. Sutherland hoped they had managed to shoot their way out, but he doubted it. He had plenty of problems of his own.

He moved to the rendezvous he had arranged with Allot. There was no sign of the latter. Sutherland waited. Nothing happened for twenty-four hours. Then to his dismay he saw a substantial party of soldiers heading in his direction. Soon there were others. They noted that there were civilians with them, so presumably these were guides who knew the area backwards.

Subsequently he learnt that Allot and his entire party had been captured as they left the airfield. Fortunately they had already laid their charges and the mission was a complete success, but the Germans and Italians now had a very quick response drill to counter these sabotage attacks – and it had been all too successful. Among those captured were Greek guides who had been methodically tortured to make them disclose the route and plans of the entire party. Surmising that Sutherland would be waiting at the rendezvous, the soldiers had now come to look for him. Sutherland and Duggan moved further up the hill; the soldiers looking for them came very close indeed.

From the height they had now reached they could see well out to sea. To their horror they saw an Italian MTB towing the boat on which they had planned to make their escape from the island. The fact that Sutherland and Duggan had now had no food for three days did not improve matters.

However, they were alive and unwounded. The search was continuing. Sutherland's only hope was to reach the submarine which should now be lying off the coast. At dusk they moved cautiously down to the beach. Here they had their first stroke of luck for a long time. The search parties had apparently been called back or were now in a different area. Using a torch which he had managed to retain through all these difficult circumstances, Sutherland flashed a signal out to sea; he hoped it would not be seen by a passing German or Italian craft. Apparently is was not, but the only response was a very faint glimmer. They waited, and tried again. This time the reply was stronger. The submarine was now nearer the surface and would presumably be looking for their boat. Sutherland sent a final signal: 'Swimming – come in.'

This was an awkward time for everyone. The submarine had the difficult task of finding swimmers in the dark while at the same time avoiding being seen itself or going aground. The coastline was virtually uncharted and was undoubtedly rocky. The swimmers had now been for five days without food and two days without water. They swam out to sea for one and a half miles. If they were not picked up they would not have the strength to swim back. Once they heard engines but they were receding and finally died away. Fortunately the submarine was circling and spotted them. They were picked up just before the submarine (HMS *Traveller*) was the target of several depth charges. The engines they had heard belonged to an Italian destroyer which had either seen their light or suspected a submarine might be hovering near. How Sutherland, who was now suffering from a severe virus infection as well as exposure, exhaustion and starvation, survived it all, no one quite knows; Scots can be very determined. Some consolation for the discomfort and heavy losses sustained by the SBS on this occasion was the fact that both the airfields were out of commission for several weeks.

While this was going on a companion raid was being staged on Tobruk harbour. Although it was primarily a SAS operation, the SBS played a prominent part – astonishingly prominent in the event. The SAS was now organized in four squadrons, A, B, C, and D. D, which included both Jellicoe and Langton, was the sea arm and included all the remaining SBS and some Greeks from the Sacred Squadron.

It was later realized that this occasion at Tobruk was not the right type of raid for the SAS or SBS. The concept was bold: it involved a sea attack using two destroyers and various torpedo boats, and a land attack with a force made up from several units in addition to the SAS. The land party was meant to simulate a party of three lorry loads of British prisoners of war escorted by German guards. It was thought that they would be able to enter the harbour area without difficulty and get to work. Meanwhile the shore parties would come in and mayhem would be let loose.

Langton's job was to signal to the MTBs, and then to direct their occupants to suitable targets. But hitches in the original plan soon began to appear: subsequently it was learnt that the Germans had been warned of the raid from a spy who had pretended to be an anti-Nazi and had eventually been allowed to join the anti-Nazi group (see below). The RAF had agreed to bomb certain specified targets but the moment their engines were heard searchlights were switched on everywhere: the landing which should have been in the dark was brightly illuminated. The MTBs came in, but the fire from the German shore defence was so fierce that only two got through and these only managed it by coming in at full speed and beaching themselves. Langton realized that no one else was likely to come in to land, but left his torch in a position where it would still act as a marker before going to find out what had happened and generally assist where needed.

Along the beach he found one of the MTBs, damaged but apparently still seaworthy although its engine would not start. Here he was joined by several other members of the SBS who had been briefed to find a boat which was still usable. However, no one could start this one up, nor would it have been likely to have travelled far if they had got it afloat as it was badly damaged. Nearby was an assault boat which had been towed in or drifted ashore. Assault craft are often less formid-able than they sound: this one consisted of a wooden floor with canvas sides held up by narrow wooden struts; it had no outboard engine but it did have paddles. All five of the SBS now climbed aboard and did a circuit of the bay. Even the most talented oarsmen cannot make an unwieldly canvas assault boat move fast, and the fact that they were never hit by German rifle fire seemed a miracle: perhaps the Germans were so astonished to see such a peculiar target that they could not aim straight. But Langton's purpose was serious enough: what he wished to discover was the progress of the raid. He could observe skirmishes between isolated bands of British and German troops, and occasionally there was the encouraging sound of heavy explosions further inland which suggested that the raiders had reached their targets. But the cost seemed to have been inordinately high. Out at sea the two destroyers were in trouble. One was towing the other and both were under fire from shore batteries. No more help could be expected from the Navy.

Langton now decided to conduct a shore reconnaissance. He found a suitable landing point, pulled the boat up on the sand, and moved inland. Almost at once they came on to a minefield. This they skirted with difficulty. Minefields were usually marked, and sometimes warning signs were put up in places where there were no mines; if you saw a notice saying, 'Beware Mines' or 'Achtung Minen' it *might* be safe to cross it. Equally it might not, and it would not be a mistake you would be likely to repeat.

Tobruk had a miscellany of former defences. At the start of the war it had been an Italian base and by the end of 1940 was a tempting target for Commando raids. In 1941, when General Sir Richard O'Connor was conducting a vigorous offensive, Tobruk was captured by the Australians who took 25,000 Italian soldiers prisoner there on 22nd January 1941. Tobruk was not left in peace for long: on 31st March Rommel and his Afrika Korps came on to the offensive. At this time the troops which Wavell had sent to Greece would have been invaluable. However, although Rommel's panzers swept by and around Tobruk they did not succeed in capturing it. Several attempts were made to roll the Germans back and to relieve Tobruk, but they did not succeed till the following November. By then Tobruk, in its besieged state, had unfortunately become a symbol of embattled resistance. For prestige reasons it was important that it should hold out and eventually be relieved, but this was not a priority which the desert commanders at the time, Generals Wavell and Auchinleck, rated very highly. Tobruk would have been a useful supply base if our armies had moved much further west, but in the seesaw fighting which was going on it locked up too many troops. The Navy found Tobruk a considerable liability, for it took them too close for too long to the nearby German Luftwaffe.

The privations of those who were besieged in Tobruk now seem to have been unnecessary but inevitable. Once we had captured the base from the Italians and filled it with supplies we could not simply evacuate it, even though it was of no tactical value. It was not the impregnable fortress it was supposed to be, a fact which was well demonstrated when Rommel captured it in a swift move on 21st June 1942. It was regained by Montgomery on 13th November when Rommel was retreating after the third battle of Alamein.

The object of the raid under discussion was to harass the German garrison, develop our raiding technique and blow up the numerous store dumps there. Many of the dumps contained British stocks from the previous period of occupation and these were undoubtedly benefitting the German war effort.

In theory we should have known the area minutely, but however well you ought to know an area it looks very different at night when occupied by the enemy. This fact was conveyed to Langton when he moved a little further inland and came upon twenty British soldiers in a wadi (dried up watercourse): these were the survivors of the land party which had been led by Lt Col Haselden. Haselden had been killed leading a charge, but his forces had inflicted considerable damage and caused many casualties before that happened.

As there was no hope of being picked up from the shore, and the whole base was buzzing with German soldiers looking for the survivors of the raiding party, it seemed an appropriate moment to depart. The survivors split into small groups and set to *walk* from Tobruk to the nearest British position, which was in Egypt, or until they encountered British forces such as the LRDG in the desert. Their chances of success in either venture did not seem great, and in fact only four reached safety; the remainder were taken prisoner by the Germans.

The four who succeeded were Langton, Cpl Wilson, Private

Watler, and Cpl Steiner, one of Captain Buck's patrol who had assumed the name 'Private Hillman' in case he should be captured. Captain Buck's force was known as the Special Interrogation Group (SIG) and was composed of Germans with anti-Nazi views. Watler would figure in other almost unbelievable escapes later. Eventually he was given the nickname by the Press of 'The man the Germans could not hold': he found it annoying and embarrassing, and threatened to punch on the nose anyone he heard using it. He was killed in an accident some years after the war.

The first part of their 400-mile walk – which took them 78 days – was the worst, for they had very little food or water, had to try to sleep by day and travel by night, and were constantly having to change direction to avoid German or Italian patrols. After a few days, when their supplies of food and water were exhausted, they went into an Arab village and were there fed and given water. The Arabs, who were not generally popular with British troops in the desert, behaved exceptionally well: not only did they shelter them, they also recommended other friendly Arab villages as staging points. Without this the party could not have succeeded. Even with it the walk was difficult enough: they finished almost bare-footed. The friendliness of these Arabs was largely due to the fact that the member of the SIG whom they had with them spoke fluent Arabic, which he had learnt in Syria; this was the Austrian, Cpl Steiner. When he approached the Arabs his accent reassured them. They had good reasons to be suspicious: Italians in disguise had been approaching Arab villages pretending to be escaped British soldiers. If the Arabs helped them, the village would be blacklisted by the Italians and destroyed.

If Langton and his companions had been able to take a direct route it would probably have been three hundred miles, not four. They had to change direction to avoid German and Italian patrols and routes, and as they had left long before the October victory at Alamein, they had no idea of the course of the war. They feared that the Germans might be already outside Cairo. To make sure they were not recaptured they went south of Alamein and into the Qattara Depression, a vast, almost impassable sand sea with a thin crust on top. Twice they heard soldiers and made detours – later they discovered these had been our troops.

This phenomenal feat of endurance was in accord with SAS/SBS philosophy as laid down by Stirling at the beginning: Whatever the task, swimming, parachuting, canoeing, crossing the desert, surviving without food or water, all these could be done better by trained and *highly motivated* men (or women).

Langton was not a man to give up – ever. At the outbreak of war he had joined the Navy but, finding himself slightly colour blind, had transferred to the Army. On being commissioned he had promptly volunteered for the Commandos. When Langton was disbanded he joined the early SBS on HMS *Medway* at Alexandria. There he learnt how to embark in canoes from submarines, for which they used an aged submarine which had escaped from Yugoslavia. After the events recorded in this book he was posted home to England for a period of recuperation, after which he joined 1 SAS for the north-west Europe campaign.

After the war he preserved his interest in rowing and took up Rugby football again playing for Richmond. It was felt, not only by Richmond who might perhaps be thought to be partisan, that if Langton had chosen to play Rugby football in his earlier career in preference to rowing, he would probably have become an International. There were others who thought that Langton had rather overdone it. Rowing men, they said, should be content to sit in a boat and become muscle-bound. Rescuing drowning men, walking through 400 miles of desert and, after all that, playing first-class Rugby football, was a bit much. Langton, always amiable, would doubtless agree.*

However, the scene was now changing. After the October/November battle of Alamein (the third) Rommel began a long retreat which left both Tobruk and Benghazi in our hands. Furthermore, 1st Army, a mixed British and American force (scarcely of Army strength) had landed in Algeria. The Germans were quickly alive to this new threat and began pouring in reinforcements: they still controlled a huge area.

* See Appendix VI

Then to everyone's astonishment the unbelievable happened. In January 1943 David Stirling, who was engaged in a deep raid into enemy territory, was captured. He escaped but was recaptured. Soon he was in Colditz (in spite of some other attempts to slip away from his captors) and a reappraisal of the future of the SBS and SAS was clearly necessary.

So far, the SAS operating with the Eighth Army was known as 1 SAS: this incorporated the SBS. A second SAS regiment had been found to operate with 1st Army: this was commanded by Lt Col William Stirling, David's brother and a veteran of many Commando raids. The presence of the Stirlings as Commanding Officers led to a pretty little riddle. What does SAS stand for? Why Stirling and Stirling, of course.

But now there was only one Stirling, and David's position was taken over by Lt Col R. B. Mayne. 'Paddy' Mayne was an Irish Rugby Football International and a tough man by any standards. Eventually he was given a DSO and *three* bars, which is equivalent to winning it three more times. He was a powerful boxer and a very quick thinker, but he was not a David Stirling: no one was. Stirling knew exactly what was happening, what was needed, what should happen next. Unfortunately he kept it all in his head, and when he went the role of the SAS was not clearly defined. Not for another year would the regiment be put on a formal basis as SAS Brigade, consisting of five regiments. Meanwhile there was plenty to be done with the knowledge and experience already gained. In order to give everyone the best outlet for his talents 2 SAS would continue in its present state and be involved in raiding in Sicily and Italy, 1 SAS would become Special Raiding Squadron and would also raid in Sicily and Italy, and the Special Boat Section (D Squadron as we noted earlier) would now be the Special Boat Squadron. Mayne would command the SAS and Jellicoe would take over the SBS. Both SAS and SBS would continue to wear the sand coloured beret and the wings of the SAS. Ultimate responsibility for the two units would be in the hands of Colonel H. J. Cator.

CHAPTER 5

Around the Islands

At this point the stories of the Special Air Service and the Special Boat Squadron diverge. We continue the story of the latter by rejoining them at Athlit, just south of Haifa. With Major the Earl Jellicoe, DSO, in command, it was divided into three detachments, L, M and S. The reason these letters were chosen rather than A, B and C which would have been more normal, was that the initials were the first letters of the names of the Detachment Commanders: L was Langton's, S was Sutherland's and M was allotted to Fitzroy Maclean. Fitzroy Maclean, whose further story was subsequently told in his book *Eastern Approaches*, had arrived from Persia (Iran) where he had been training a carefully selected body of men. The total strength of the SBS was now 230. Each detachment commander had approximately sixty men at his disposal. Two newcomers also joined the unit. The presence of these two would have far-reaching effects: one was Anders Lassen, a Dane who would eventually be awarded a posthumous VC. It is unusual to be awarded a VC and still more so if you are a foreigner serving in the British Army. Curiously enough, the only two VCs ever awarded to foreigners serving in the British Army have both been given to Danes.

Both these new recruits came from 62 Commando. 62 Commando had had a brief existence under the command of Captain Gustavus March Phillips, ably assisted by Captain Geoffrey Appleyard. It had performed invaluable services in cross-Channel raiding, landing and collecting agents, and so on. March Phillips was killed in a raid on Port-en-Bessin, Normandy in November 1942. Appleyard took over his duties, but when the Commandos were reorganized 62 was disbanded and its members distributed to other units. Appleyard went to 2 SAS and was later killed in a plane crash in Sicily.

Lassen was a tall, fair Dane with very light blue eyes. He was amiable and cheerful but sometimes if you caught a glance from those eyes you might feel relieved he was on your side and not an enemy. Although of an aristocratic family he had gone to sea in 1939 as an ordinary seaman. He then volunteered to return to Denmark for 'special duties', which meant sabotage and spying on the Germans. He was sent to Scotland for training but was thought to be better suited to Commando work than spying. He proved very successful and, after a particularly brilliant exploit against German shipping off the West African coast, was commissioned. He took his promotion lightly and never wore his rank badges or the Military Cross he had been awarded unless directly ordered to do so.

With Lassen came Philip Pinckney. Pinckney had gone to Trinity College, Cambridge after leaving Eton, but he preferred bird-watching in the fens to work and left Cambridge after a year to go out to India as a tea-broker instead. When war broke out Pinckney joined up and soon found himself in the Commandos. He was outstandingly brave but tended to be casual. Once on an exercise on Salisbury Plain he attacked the wrong target: the wrong target happened to be a regular regiment in a high state of awareness, and when Pinckney tried to overcome the sentry he received a bayonet wound in his arm. The sentry was promoted. When in North Africa he was inclined to wander into dinner in an open-necked shirt. A message was sent to him: 'The Commanding Officer wishes Captain Pinckney to wear a tie for dinner.' When all had assembled for dinner it was thought that Pinckney had decided not to dine but, at the last moment, he appeared stark naked except for a beautifully tied tie. Thus attired he dined perfectly normally. His Commanding Officer thought it was quite a good joke, but Pinckney did not repeat it.

His most valuable contribution to the SBS, and in turn to the SAS, was his interest in survival foods. Many of these were reasonably orthodox but some were not. He tried out everything personally: twigs, grasses, slugs, snails, leaves, insects. Some of the latter were so repulsive that men could scarcely bear to look at them, but he munched them up in a spirit of scientific curiosity. Bizarre though it all seemed, it was the foundation for the expertise which enables to-day's explorer or soldier to live longer in conditions in which his predecessor might have died. Pinckney, sadly, did not stay with the SBS long. He went off to 2 SAS and was parachuted into Italy for sabotage behind the enemy lines. On 10th July 1943 he jumped on another raid, although he already had a cracked spine. He was captured and, although in uniform, was shot as a spy.

It might be asked how, when so many millions of men were involved in the war a tiny unit like the SBS could have any effect, or indeed justify its existence. It is a valid question, the answer to which will become apparent in the following pages.

At this stage in the war it seemed as if the tide might be turning slightly in favour of the Allies, but there was undoubtedly much more turning needed before victory could be remotely in sight. Deep in Russia the Germans had had reverses, notably at Stalingrad, but these made them more determined. They still held Europe from the Arctic Circle to the Eastern Mediterranean. They had lost the battle for Africa, and 250,000 Germans and Italians had been taken prisoner in Tunisia. But winning battles in Africa could not win wars in Europe, even though losing there might not have done much to assist a final German victory. The Japanese had also apparently reached the limit of their abilities at runaway conquest, having been checked and pushed back in Burma and having lost the valuable base at Guadalcanal. Their navy had also sustained heavy losses, and Admiral Yamamoto had been killed. But Allied shipping losses in the Atlantic had been so great that it was felt that the war might be being lost there. Hitler was still boasting about a 'secret weapon' and as it was known that German scientists were experimenting with methods of making nuclear bombs, there was no reason to suppose that time was on the side of the Allies.

Militarily, the principal fact for the Germans was that they had close on two million men locked in a death struggle with an even larger army in Russia; thousands had already been killed or died of exposure. The population of Russia was nearly four times that of Germany, and although the Germans were filling their ranks with soldiers from Bulgaria, Roumania and the like, their resources had to be conserved. When the Allies invaded

Sicily the Germans managed to extricate themselves without too much loss, but they dared not take too many German troops from Italy in case Mussolini should be deposed and the Italians tried to make a separate peace. Although there seemed as yet no danger of an immediate invasion of France, this was an avowed American intention and the western seaboard had to be held in a state of readiness. All the time Germany was being bombed.

In these circumstances the German High Command was constantly looking for ways in which manpower could be conserved and more troops found for the insatiable maw of the Russian Front. But Commando raids, SAS work, saboteurs, and groups of partisans made it impossible for the Germans to leave whole districts unguarded or the resistance and sabotage would become more widespread, more bold and better organized; unless nipped in the bud with extreme ruthlessness any form of resistance could quickly develop into a major threat. Some areas were more vulnerable than others. Yugoslavia had been comparatively easy to conquer, but looked like being increasingly difficult to hold – resistance would build up to a point when as many as twenty divisions would be needed to contest it. Hitler was personally very apprehensive of an Allied landing in Norway and insisted that adequate precautions were taken. But there was another, even more serious, danger looming: the Greek islands were mainly garrisoned by Italians, and Hitler suspected that the Allies might be planning an assault to recapture them. This could have been very dangerous indeed. With the Greek islands in Allied hands, pressure could be put on Turkey to join their side and the whole of what Churchill used to refer to as 'the soft underbelly of Europe' could be exposed. Hard-pressed though Germany was to provide troops for all her far-flung commitments, the loss of the Greek islands could not be permitted. Hitler decided to act.

At the same time Churchill was desperately trying to persuade the Americans to back Britain up in this area. The Americans were sceptical – to them the only way the war could be won was by an invasion of France and a drive to Berlin. All other activities seemed like sideshows or tricks of the British to reassert themselves in their former areas of influence. In vain did Churchill argue that a thrust up through the Greek islands and through Bulgaria could continue into Roumania and cut off the principal supply base of German oil; the Americans shied away from any involvement in what were known as the Balkans. Exasperating and disastrous as this attitude was (for the Russians eventually took Bulgaria and Roumania under their control and have never relinquished them) it is understandable. The Americans viewed European politics with much the same suspicion as we British regard Central American politics; if you get involved you may well burn your fingers all to no avail. In addition, Admiral King was strongly anti-British and was not prepared to let the American naval forces under his command play what he thought of as a typically British game. It is now obvious, with hindsight, that the Greek islands should have been regarded as one of the vital strategic points of the war; as it was, they were lost to the enemy all too easily.

The sequence of events reads like a chapter of accidents as far as the Allied war effort was concerned. The SBS, as we have seen, had previously been employed in the Western Mediterranean although Crete had also been raided. After Sicily had been captured and Italy invaded, and SBS and 2 SAS had been allotted to the Italian mainland as an operational area, the obvious area for the SBS was the Greek islands which were garrisoned by Italian and Germans. The Germans were making use of their facilities, but control rested with the Italians.

However, soon after the invasion of Italy Marshal Badoglio signed a peace treaty with the Allies on behalf of the Italian King Victor Emmunel III. Mussolini was imprisoned; four battleships and six cruisers of the Italian fleet sailed to Malta and surrendered.

Hitler had been expecting this for some time, and took precautions to see that those parts of Italy still under German influence were not allowed to surrender. The Germans then fought a long and gruelling campaign to retain their hold on Italy as long as possible. In a daring raid Mussolini was snatched back and reinstated by the Germans. Italy is a land which favours defenders, but the tenacity shown by the Germans was a surprise to everyone, probably even themselves. Bitter and bloody though the campaign was on the Italian front, and it lasted two years, it was always regarded as a secondary front by the Allies. It was unlikely that the Allied armies would ever thrust up through Italy to Berlin; France would be the only 'second front' worth mentioning. This view, combined with Communist-inspired demands to 'open the Second Front now' (long before adequate preparations had been completed) made those who had already opened second fronts in Africa, Sicily, and Italy a little irritated.

When Italy was trying to surrender, the Greek islands were a peach ripe for plucking. In spite of a German presence, the Italians on the islands might be induced to surrender if given the impression that the Allies were going to appear in force. Hitler and the German High Command were only too well aware of that possibility and took prompt steps to prevent it. Owing to the inadequate Allied forces for capturing this rich prize, the Germans were able to retain the islands and take many British prisoners in the process.

The only saving grace in this tale of missed chances was provided by the SBS. Once the Germans were fully in control the SBS began to harass them. So effective were the SBS efforts that the Germans had to keep six divisions in the islands. Those six divisions would have been useful in Italy, but even more useful on the French coast when D Day came. The claim that some 230 men could tie down six divisions (about 90,000 men) may seem an exaggeration. In other areas, the 230 would not have lasted more than a month, but the Greek islands with their jagged coasts, rugged terrain and almost inaccessible retreats were highly favourable to guerrillas co-operating with people who possessed local knowledge. There are two other points which need a mention. One is that the sort of person who can take part in hit and run raiding is a rare breed; many like to try, but few succeed. The second is that the local population must be on your side. With the help of the local population the guerrilla – whether rural, naval or urban – can continue for a long time. His luck will run out if he is betrayed or if people among whom he has his base become weary of searching and reprisals and begin to lose sympathy. Then his sources of food, shelter and intelligence may be denied him and his work totally invalidated even if he is not actually betrayed.

In order to give the setting for the next phase of SBS activities we have ranged ahead. We left the regiment training for its new rôle. Its latest acquisition, Captain Fitzroy Maclean, did not stay long. In July he was whisked away to create deep trouble for the Germans who were endeavouring to control Yugoslavia. Maclean was no newcomer either to the SAS or guerrilla work: he had taken part in the earlier SAS raids, and once when challenged by a German sentry had rebuked him in German for slackness and inefficiency – with the man suitably humbled, he had proceeded on his way.

Maclean's command was now taken by Captain J. N. Lapraik, MC. Lapraik was eventually awarded a DSO, an OBE, and another bar to his MC. He was a very successful middle distance runner and swimmer. It was difficult to believe that at the age of seven he had been completely crippled by tuberculosis of the knee and had had to spend years with his leg in plaster. He had been a cripple for five years in all, but once he began to recover had never stopped building up health and endurance. Lapraik's training was renowned for its toughness, but no one could or would wish to complain. It had worked for a man who had spent five years of his life as a cripple: it should therefore work for anyone else.*

The SBS opened their 1943 attack on the Greek islands with another excursion to Crete. The position of Crete, well to the south of the group, made it extremely useful to the Germans who were bent on harassing Mediterranean shipping, but its valuable tactical position was likely to prove a liability if they were forced to retreat.

Inevitably Sutherland, with his previous experience of the island, was chosen for this assignment. Once again the aim was the destruction of airfields. On this occasion Sutherland was accompanied by Lassen and Lamonby as well as Lt Rowe, a former Oxford rowing blue. Rowe was allotted Timbaki airfield, but was disappointed to find it was deserted. Lamonby had an almost equally frustrating experience at Heraklion where there were no aircraft, but cheered up when he discovered a petrol dump. He blew it up.

* See Appendix V for further details of Lapraik

Lassen's patrol set out for Kastelli, where they had the encouraging sight of eight Stukas, five Junkers 88s and other miscellaneous aircraft including fighters. Lassen looked distinctly cheerful. His optimism was not diminished by the people living in the area who were friendly if discouraging. According to their information – and some of them worked on the airfield – the aircraft were closely guarded day and night.

The main attack took place on 24th June. Lassen cut a hole in the wire and walked around to see for himself. The observation of the local people seemed to have some validity. There were numerous sentries and they all seemed alert. Claiming to be a German officer, he negotiated three of them without difficulty and had just arrived at the fourth when one of the earlier ones had second thoughts and fired a warning shot. His fellow sentry then started to arrest Lassen but Lassen shot him before the process could get very far.

Lassen now took 'evasive action'. Slipping away in the darkness was no problem. After a short time he threw several grenades to create a diversion on one side of the airfield while he himself went to the other to lay bombs on planes which had been left unguarded in the general confusion and uproar – Lassen's ability to appear and disappear would cause much trouble to many other Germans and Italians in the future. He then left the airfield. When laying up the next day he was observed by some Cretans who decided to earn a reward from the Germans. Lassen, though exhausted, was alert and when he saw German soldiers climbing up to where he was hiding he hastily changed his position. In order to throw off the pursuit he had to remain in the mountains for three days without food before returning hungry but unscathed to the party's rendezvous.

Lassen had been accompanied by Sgt Nicholson and Cpl Greaves. They had cut into the airfield on the opposite side to him and had immediately begun looking for targets. They too ran into sentries but, perhaps more wisely than Lassen, dashed off into the darkness rather than fighting it out and creating too much noise. A shouting sentry was one thing, but an exchange of shots was another matter entirely and would draw men to the spot like wasps to jam. By this time Lassen's activities on his side of the airfield were making all the sentries jumpy and distracted, and instead of concentrating on their main task of guarding the aircraft they began to talk agitatedly with each other. Profiting from this diversion, Nicholson and Greaves placed bombs on several aircraft and a petrol supply point. It was now time to leave. They were lucky in finding a piece of the perimeter wire unattended, and they made their way through it. On the way back to the rendezvous they were nearly caught several times before throwing off the pursuers.

Getting on to the island had been comparatively easy; getting off it looked like being extremely difficult. Not least of their problems was the fact that a number of Cretans had seen them and decided to join them. These Cretans were far too untrained and undisciplined to be anything but an embarrassment, but for diplomatic reasons it was not possible to be rid of them. Cairo radio had reported the raid and announced that all the raiders had returned safely, but the Germans and Italians had their doubts. Instead of wasting efforts by searching the hills they concentrated around the possible get-away points. They divided their forces into very small patrols and methodically watched chosen areas. Clashes were inevitable; in one, Lamonby was killed: he had killed a German a second earlier. He was the only British casualty; the others were picked up by a motor launch and took two German prisoners with them.

This gave rise to a somewhat bizarre incident. When they reached Cairo and were heading for GHQ they passed Groppi's, famous for its tea, ice-cream and elegant staff officers who were nicknamed 'Groppi's Horse'. It seemed a good place to stop for a cool drink before being debriefed at GHQ, so Sutherland and Lassen decided to call in. But they had the two German POWs with them and could scarcely leave them in the truck outside unguarded. They took them inside and bought them ice-creams. There was such a variety of uniforms to be seen in Groppi's that even two German ones might have passed unnoticed. Unfortunately it did not. One of Groppi's Horse was being unusually efficient and reported this strange quartet: subsequently Sutherland was reprimanded.

When it was known that Italy was about to surrender it became urgently necessary to acquire Rhodes before the Germans could put in a stronger claim. The island was nominally under the control of an Italian governor, Admiral Campioni. GHQ Cairo thought that Campioni might be persuaded to surrender the island and avoid much bloodshed, but speed was clearly necessary. A day had already been lost, for the plan had been that contact should be made with Campioni the day before the Armistice; unfortunately bad weather had prevented this.

The person appointed to handle these delicate negotiations was Jellicoe himself. If Campioni was not impressed by an English aristocrat, son of one of the most famous admirals of all time, he must be a very dull character indeed. However Campioni knew something which the British did not: the Germans had 10,000 troops on the island and these were unlikely to surrender weakly. Campioni suspected that they were likely to kidnap or kill him. Jellicoe did not know this. He set off on the 9th September in a Halifax bomber and dropped near Marizza accompanied by an interpreter, Major Dolbey and a signaller, Sergeant Kesterton.

The weather was little improved from the previous night. Dolbey had never parachuted in his life and displayed considerable courage from first to last in the enterprise. He needed it. He landed on the tarmac surface of a main road, an experience that could have proved disastrous for even the most experienced parachutist; the fall broke his leg. Jellicoe and Kesterton had an uncomfortable though less disastrous arrival. The Italians, having seen the parachutes, opened fire under the impression that they were Germans coming to take over the island in spite of the Armistice. The situation was, to quote a word much used in military reports, 'confused'. Having made their descent in darkness on to an unknown area they had now become separated and lost.

But the Italians soon had search parties out looking for them. The first to be discovered, fortunately, was Dolbey. He explained who they were, and why they had arrived in that somewhat surprising fashion. Kesterton and Jellicoe had been blown well away from the intended dropping zone and had both had rough landings. Jellicoe suspected that he had drifted into the part of the island where the Germans were concentrated. He was carrying a letter from General Wilson, C in C

Mediterranean, to Admiral Campioni, strongly recommending surrender to the British. Jellicoe, realizing that disaster would follow if the letter fell into German hands, decided to eat it. Unfortunately the letter had been meant to impress Campioni not only by its contents but also by its official appearance. This made it extremely inedible and it took him nearly an hour to chew it up. The effect was to give him a raging thirst which lasted for 24 hours. The Italian search parties soon found Jellicoe and Kesterton and welcomed them. Dolbey was sent for hospital attention: Jellicoe was given treatment for his thirst. Then, with surprising speed, a vehicle arrived to take them to Admiral Campioni.

The Admiral was not at his best. It was 2 a.m. He had only recently heard of the Armistice himself and although he had some 30,000 Italian troops under his command they were widely dispersed. The 10,000 Germans, on the other hand, were concentrated – and close by – or so he thought. Actually, the situation was worse than he suspected. The Germans, who had been the first to inform him of the Armistice, had very civilly agreed that no troop movements should take place. They had immediately deployed their forces, occupying the principal airfields. It was fortunate for the SBS that they had not landed at Marizza or they would have encountered unfriendly Germans. The Italians were resisting this German takeover, but as they had mostly been caught unprepared Campioni did not feel they were ultimately likely to be very successful. It was vital that British troops should arrive quickly to assist the Italians. Pressed to define what and when the British reinforcements would be, Jellicoe was in a difficult position. Dolbey, lying on a stretcher and in some pain from his broken leg, was endeavouring to translate the somewhat delicate exchanges and managed very well in the circumstances. Jellicoe knew only too well that the first available reinforcements would consist of Sutherland and his detachment who had come up to Castelrosso, but did not think that sixty more men was a figure likely to inspire much confidence in the Admiral. He indicated that larger contingents of troops would be likely to arrive within a week.

This time lag was no encouragement to Campioni, but he did not wish to offend the Allies or to break the terms of the

Armistice. However, he did not wish to be removed to an internment camp in Germany, which might well be his fate if he helped the British and then discovered that the reinforcements did not turn up in time to protect him from the Germans. He behaved very well in the circumstances, allowing Jellicoe use of his own radio station to obtain further instructions from GHQ Cairo. As the Germans would undoubtedly be monitoring signals traffic, this was a generous gesture. But he insisted that his three unexpected guests should all take off their uniforms and put on civilian clothes.

The Germans now explained very forcefully to Campioni that if he disregarded the Armistice and co-operated with them his future would be comfortable and ensured. If, however, he decided to throw in his lot with the British, who had no troops to back their brave words, the Germans might have to take him under their own protection. Jellicoe was cheered to learn that another detachment of SBS were now to come to Rhodes via Simi. He informed Campioni of this encouraging news, hoping it would be taken as a sign of better things to come.

Campioni's dilemma was still unresolved. The Germans were deploying all over the island and the Italians were unable or unwilling to do much to stop them. When the movements had reached what the Germans felt was a satisfactory stage they informed Campioni, and added that they were about to take over the township of Rhodes itself. Unless Campioni broke off negotiations with the British they could see no way of preventing this. Campioni informed Jellicoe that the other SBS must not come any nearer than Simi and that Jellicoe and his companions, suitably disguised as civilians, should join them there; if at some time in the near future the Allies could arrive with adequate forces Campioni would be glad to welcome them. He went even further: to assist the Allies he allowed his own Chief of Staff, one Colonel Fanetza, to accompany Jellicoe. Fanetza could then put his specialized knowledge of the island's defences and the German disposition at the disposal of GHQ Cairo. It was a generous offer, but it went wrong. They left on an Italian motor launch and reached Castelrosso. Unfortunately, as they stepped off the launch Fanetza missed his footing and disappeared into the somewhat unattractive water by the jetty. Jellicoe thought this was quite amusing but his view was not shared by Fanetza, and while Jellicoe was otherwise engaged Fanetza ordered the captain of the launch to return with him to Rhodes, saying this was under Campioni's orders. He must have prided himself on his foresight for he arrived to find that Campioni had now agreed that Rhodes should be put under German command. The news reached Jellicoe who was not pleased; his immediate reaction was to take steps to ensure that the Germans were denied similar success with the other islands. He had little enough to prevent it, as his total strength of effectiveness was fifty-five. With these, and a few launches, he set himself the task of taking over the remainder of the Dodecanese islands one by one.

It was a situation in which speed and bluff were the most important factors. Where the islands had Italian garrisons the occupants were easily persuaded to throw in their lot with the British, but where there was a German garrison, however small, or where there was a German garrison on a neighbouring island, it was a different story. Fortunately there were a number of islands with Italian garrisons and some islands with no garrisons at all. Among the Italian-held islands taken over by the British were Leros, Cos, Simi and Castelrosso. Jellicoe thought there might be problems at Cos when he saw that Colonel Fanetza was on very friendly terms with the Governor, but the Governor duly handed over the island.

The next stage in the battle for the Dodecanese looked like being more active. Although Jellicoe had arranged for landing grounds to be available on the islands which he visited, there was no real assurance that there would be enough troops available to make use of them. On the other hand it seemed very likely that the Germans would make full use of the facilities they possessed on Rhodes: as we have seen those facilities included three very useful airfields.

The first British move was to add to the forces on Cos. Here a battalion of the Buffs and a battalion of the Royal West Kent Regiment were quickly installed. Some more SBS, commanded by Lapraik and including Lassen, arrived in Simi. The Italian garrison was small, numbering 140, but seemed ready to co-operate with the British force. Lapraik quickly realized that his command would require diplomacy as well as military skill. Most of the island's inhabitants were Greek and they hated the Italians. By the time Lapraik arrived there was a long backlog of insults to be avenged, grievances to be resolved, and wrongs to be righted. If the SBS left the islands, the Greeks affirmed, it would be a bad day indeed for the Italians. Lapraik was diplomatic but firm; as soon as possible he delegated the task of civil administration to someone else and set about planning raids on Rhodes. He acquired six caïques, which he manned with mixed SBS and Greek crews. For preliminary reconnaissance on Rhodes he sent Lt Stellin, a New Zealander. Stellin remained on Rhodes for nearly a month in all, during which time he had some very narrow escapes. He noted that Calchi, which is only twelve miles from Rhodes, was so far ungarrisoned by the Germans. To ensure that it should not now become a German outpost too easily Lassen was sent there to encourage local resistance. Lassen did this by strengthening the defences and generally being so warlike that the local police in charge of the defence of the island were more frightened of Lassen than they were of any German threat, then he returned to Simi. Soon afterwards, having observed signs of activity and experienced raids from Calchi, the Germans arrived and were surprised at the intensity of the resistance. They took over the island but sustained a number of casualties in doing so.

The battle for the islands depended on a peculiar equation. The British had transport but very few men: the Germans had more men but very little transport. It was interesting to learn after the war that the Germans had at first decided that, Rhodes excepted, the Dodecanese could not be retained. Admiral Doenitz felt that the Germans already had too much on their hands in suppressing partisans in Greece and Yugoslavia to take on other commitments. If the Royal Navy really gave the area its attention the German shipping would simply be destroyed, and although the Germans had aircraft on Rhodes they had all too few planes elsewhere in the Mediterranean area. The Germans did not suspect that most of the Allied aircraft were being reserved for operations in Italy and that very few planes, if any, could or would be made available for defending the Dodecanese. Churchill, who had no doubts about the importance of the area, raised the subject with Roosevelt over and over again but received a dusty answer. The British Commander-in-Chief Mediterranean, General Wilson, who also had no illusions about the importance of the islands, scoured his resources to see what could be spared for establishing a firm presence there.

Hitler was well aware of German deficiencies in the area but felt that for reasons of political prestige he must defy the gloomy advice of his commanders. He therefore ordered that the islands would be held, even though it meant taking aircraft from France, diverting aircraft which would otherwise have gone to the Russian front, and detailing shipping from the Adriatic. All this would no doubt impress the Turks and convince them of German resolve and eventual success: Hitler was well aware that the Allies were trying to draw Turkey into the war on their side. Turkey had no wish to be drawn into the war on anyone's side, but in order not to offend anyone she turned a blind eye to the numerous infringements of her neutrality. Most of these came from the Allied side as Turkish territorial waters and airspace were often used by British military forces. Hitler was not unaware of this and knew that, although the Turks were apprehensive of a German alliance, they were even more apprehensive of German aircraft bombing Turkish cities. Nor were the Turks too unhappy at the Germans putting their ancient enemy, Russia, under pressure: it would be bad enough to have a German army of occupation in Turkey, but it would be worse to have a Russian one. Hitler was aware just what a peculiar mental tightrope the Turks were treading, so he ordered his aircraft not to bomb British shipping in Turkish waters however flagrant their violation of neutrality. However, he could see that if Germany evacuated the islands, including Rhodes, Turkish 'neutrality' to the Allies might easily become full-time co-operation.

Hitler probably underestimated the problems the British would have if and when he decided to make a full scale attack on the islands. Both Hitler and the Allies overestimated the resources the Italians had established around their garrison; these did not include enough larger weapons of the type which might have been expected. The Allies had eight destroyers and six submarines, but neither these nor the ground forces could be provided with adequate air cover. Most of the RAF bases were over three hundred miles away and any fighters or ground support aircraft from these would be opposed by the formidable Messerschmidt 109-Gs which would be based in Greece, Crete or Rhodes. These were the odds which the SBS and the small British forces would be facing. The SBS had made a very promising start, and whatever happened they would be a thorn in the German flesh, but undoubtedly the situation would get worse before it got better. Even when the worst came to the worst, as it did, the saving grace was that the Germans had to lock up in those islands divisions which they desperately needed to use elsewhere.

This is running slightly ahead of the story but it underlines the fact that if raiding forces are active, effective and persistent, they immobilize enemy troops. The enemy troops may be active in looking for the raiders and endeavouring to eliminate them by every form of ruthlessness they can bring to bear, but as long as the raiders are effective the occupying force cannot withdraw without losing diplomatic and military prestige.

In September Sutherland moved from Cos to Samos, where his detachment received a rapturous welcome. The Greeks, who had no love for their recent Italian masters, suggested that these should now all be massacred. Sutherland found himself unable to agree although later, when an Italian Blackshirt battalion with strong Fascist ideas proved uncooperative, he might have wished he had been less firm.

Lapraik's detachment had now begun work on Rhodes. Lassen's legacy on Calchi had been that the islanders were now so determined that they were already mounting British-run operations against their larger neighbour Rhodes; they paid for this eventually, as we saw. Two men from Lapraik's detachment threaded their way through the minefields outside Rhodes and made a quick reconnaissance; other raids followed.

The battle was now warming up. The Long Range Desert Group, their work in the desert finished, had been to the Lebanon for training in mountain warfare and were now sent to demonstrate their accumulated skills in the islands. There were now British forces on Cos, Samos, Leros, Simi, Icaria,

Stampali and Castelrosso. The Germans had valuable assets in the possesion of Rhodes and Crete, and also had control of a substantial number of the smaller islands such as Lemnos, Chios, Mytilene, and Kasos. There were still unclaimed islands which could be useful. Sutherland, when relieved on Samos, went on to Kalymnos where he was joined by a detachment from the LRDG. Kalymnos, sometimes known as Calino, is four miles from Cos.

This gave the SBS a grandstand view of Cos when the Germans invaded, which they did on 2nd October. What they saw was not heartening. The island had already been bombed heavily, and the airfield at Antimachia badly damaged. When the invasion came the Germans had complete air superiority. The British forces on the island numbered 1100, and the Italians whose hearts were by no means in the forthcoming fight amounted to 4000. The Germans arrived with sufficient forces to outnumber their opponents by five to one, and their invasion force also had suitable equipment for the task.

They did not capture Cos easily. They were attacked by the Navy on the way in, and once ashore had to fight a series of gruelling battles – but the odds were too heavily in their favour for it to last long. Sutherland, seeing it happen, sent Walter Milner-Barry with his detachment to delay the inevitable as long as possible. Milner-Barry was something of a legend in the SBS. Though older than most of them, being in his forties, he still took part in the most strenuous activities. He had been in the Middle East for years, employed by Shell, and it was generally thought that what he did not know about the Mediterranean area was probably not worth knowing. Milner-Barry sized up the situation rapidly and decided that the first priority was the evacuation of people who could still be used elsewhere: he removed 105 by arranging a complicated system of journeys in small boats or on rafts.

Almost inevitably, Watler, Langton's companion on the desert walk, was on Cos. He became cut off from his patrol and after a time was captured. Being captured was not the obstacle to Watler's enterprise that it might have been to others, so he feigned malaria. It was an impressive performance and the Germans gave him time to get over the worst of it before removing him from the island with the other prisoners. He was interned in Cos castle but made a rope of the electric light wiring and let himself out. The Germans were now in force on the island and it was hardly surprising that his period of liberty ended five days later. He was put back in the castle. He looked around for more wire and two days later was at large again. This time he decided there was no settled future for him on the island, so he went to the coast and swam for two miles until he found a village which the Germans had not occupied. He then hitched a lift on a caïque but not before he had sabotaged some nearby German equipment; he had no explosives but he found that a hammer and some nails made a reasonable substitute.

The Germans now turned their attention to Simi. Here the defences had been organized by Lapraik, and the first arrival, a caïque, did not get very close. The Germans eventually managed to put a considerable number of men ashore and shouted through megaphones, telling the Italians to surrender and be forgiven. As it seemed that some might believe this somewhat improbable assurance, Lapraik sent Lassen to stiffen their resolve. Lapraik's patrol gave them a demonstration of what was required by killing three Germans and capturing three more; he told the Italians to do the same. He then took up an unaccustomed position to the rear of the Italians and informed them that any retirement would mean certain death from his pistol, whereas a courageous advance might mean victory. This well-established military formula worked very well.

But there were too many Germans with too many boats. They now held the southern ridge, so Lapraik decided to dislodge them with Bren gun fire. As this made the Germans distinctly uncomfortable it was then reinforced by a frontal attack and a flank attack, the last using Italian troops. The Germans called for aid from their Stukas, but the dive bombers failed to hit anything vital. The invaders were now evacuating the ridge and withdrawing to the beach where they waited to be collected. A number of large craft came in, including a schooner. Lapraik sent a caïque to harry this boat; it succeeded in edging it to a position where the Brens, which were proving worth considerably more than their weight in gold, were able to spray it with bullets. The defenders had won.

The total German losses were never known but were enough for them to give up the struggle. The SBS had two wounded, one killed. The Italians, who had responded extremely well to the call, had ten casualties, no one killed.

The following day the Germans returned with Stukas and pounded the island at two-hour intervals. The Italians, and particularly their commander, were now showing tremendous spirit. Two Stukas paid the price, but in one of the later attacks Lapraik's base was hit; this became the occasion of an act of great heroism and self-sacrifice. Two men were buried in the debris. They were Corporal Greeves and Private Bishop. Greeves had a heavy beam across his stomach; Bishop was trapped by his foot. An American volunteer ambulance man named Jarell had the unenviable task of explaining to Bishop that if he were removed more debris would inevitably fall on Greeves and kill him. The only solution was for Jarell to amputate Bishop's foot, without proper anaesthetics, equipment or room to move, and they would leave the foot where it was. Both could then be pulled out. Bishop immediately agreed. Sadly he died from the shock the next day and Greeves, though alive when released, died soon afterwards.

Meanwhile the battle continued. The dive bombers came back and hammered the island again. Lapraik now received orders to withdraw to Castelrosso, and although this order was countermanded almost as soon as given, it was repeated and executed. Before leaving, the garrison had the task of destroying all stores likely to be of use to the enemy.

A week later Lapraik sailed quietly back to the island to see what the Germans were up to. To his surprise he found no one there. He took a good look round and noted a site which would be ideal as a base for raiding.

Leros was the next to feel the weight of the German attack. If it fell, Samos would probably go with it, and Kalymnos too. Leros had a proper harbour but Samos had too much open coastline to be properly defensible.

David Sutherland had been sent to Leros, where it was thought there might be an invasion by air. There were already three British infantry battalions on the island and an anti-aircraft battery. There was a rumour, doubtless well founded, that the Germans had allotted a parachute battalion for the next round of operations. The SBS was required to deploy in any areas in which these airborne troops might expect to land without encountering resistance.

Invasion came on 11th November 1943, beginning with a small landing near Clidi. But this was clearly not the main attack. The remainder followed in the shape of Junkers 52s discharging six hundred parachutists. As is now well known, it is not sufficient to put a parachutist on the ground armed merely with what he carries strapped to his body. He needs supplementary ammunition, food and equipment which is dropped in containers near to the place where it is hoped the parachutist will land. Unfortunately containers and parachutists rarely if ever land in the same place, so the SBS now concentrated on keeping the parachutists away from the containers which were essential for the continuance of their fighting. On arrival the parachutists received such a concentrated fire that they temporarily abandoned their efforts to recover their containers, which they decided to rescue after nightfall. By that time the SBS had removed most of the containers and their contents were very welcome.

Another attack now came in from the sea. Grimly, the Germans fought their way ashore. The next day as dawn broke, a second contingent of parachutists was delivered to the island.

This second wave was even more unfortunate than the first. During the night the wind had got up and a gale was blowing. The heavily-loaded Junkers struggled with the gusty wind, and as some lost height four fell to ground fire. The remaining parachutists, some 200 men, then encountered a parachutist's nightmare: many of the parachutes failed to open, probably through faulty packing, and the soldiers simply plunged to the ground. Those who reached the ground safely were unable to cope with the gusts of wind which dragged them over trees, bushes and rocks as they vainly tried to release themselves. Some were blown so far off their dropping zone that they fell into the sea. Only a dozen or so arrived safely and those were either killed or surrendered. Calm once more settled on Leros.

But there were still German parachutists from the first wave up in the hills, getting very hungry, desperate and weak.

The Germans now made a final all-out effort. Attacks by Stukas became almost continuous, dive bombing or ground strafing.

Long after the war was over, when the campaigns were studied and their lessons evaluated by the generals who had grown up subsequently, it was decided that dive bombing was a comparatively ineffective form of warfare, nor was ground strafing much better. This may be so, but it was not apparent to those in France, the Greek islands, or any other hot spots. The noise of a dive bomber may not kill you but it does disturb the concentration, and troops whose every movement is observed and harassed from the air do not care much for the process. Firing at a dive bomber with a .303 rifle or even a Bren was unlikely to do much to stop it, even if it did give the defender a feeling that he was at least punching back. Nowadays with surface to air missiles and various forms of mobile aircraft-hunting rockets it is a different story and the balance of power has been much restored, but on Leros the Stukas were having it all their own way.

The Germans were not having it all their own way at sea. Owing to the scarcity of transports, the final assault could not be delivered. The British Navy was just as vulnerable to air attack as the land forces, and naval losses mounted up. The Germans now had a mixture of aircraft which included Dorniers. These high altitude bombers, which flew well above the height of the British fighters, carried a new glider bomb.

This account of what was an intense and complicated battle is necessarily shortened and does not indicate the fury of the fighting on land, sea and air. Over a thousand Germans were buried on Leros and many more died at sea in the attempts to land. British and Italian casualties were lower as would be expected with the defending force, but even so they ran into hundreds. The lesson of Leros was that the Germans used their air supremacy to get their men ashore and then to supply them, and their troops fought with great determination and skill. In the street fighting few buildings escaped damage. The SBS, deployed in the hills against parachutists and for sniping, was not concerned with the deadly struggles taking place around the harbour and the towns and was astonished to learn that the garrison had surrendered. Had the SBS been employed elsewhere on the island they would no doubt have had many more casualties than the seven they sustained. As soon as they heard the news of the surrender they prepared to evacuate, not wishing to be hunted down and taken prisoner; they took a caïque and departed the same night. One of their number, Lt K. Balsillie, had violent dysentery and was considered to be too ill to travel; he was therefore left behind. After his comrades had departed he began to improve and after a few days stole a German boat and rowed himself to Turkey – a distance of sixty miles. In view of the fact that dysentery is a disease which, apart from its other inconveniences, leaves a person as weak as a kitten, this feat of Balsillie ranks high in the SBS/SAS record.

Although the SBS contingent had got away from Leros it seemed possible that there would be other British soldiers still uncaptured on the island. To get them off, launches were sent out during the next few nights. Several dozen British soldiers were found and evacuated.

With Leros gone there was no hope of retaining Samos. Accordingly the small contingent of British and Italian troops promptly left the island. Castelrosso was our sole remaining possession in the Dodecanese. Militarily this was a serious setback and one which should have been avoided, although everyone at the time and later agreed that the Germans had displayed boldness, determination and great skill in the way in which they had handled their forces. Since their great run of victories in 1940 the Germans had made no other permanent gains, and this victory in the Aegean surprised everyone. It was, of course, on the lines of their earlier conquests: massive air superiority and great tactical skill in concentrating land forces. It was one of the last occasions when they would have local air superiority and it demonstrated how effective that can be.

The Turks had been remarkably patient in their acceptance of British ships violating their territorial waters, and now that the battle had gone to the Germans in spite of this forbearance the Turks were distinctly cooler to the Allies. For the Germans it was a Pyrrhic victory. They had sustained heavy losses in extending their commitments, and the need to garrison these new gains would be a constant drain on resources – the SBS were fully determined it would be so.

In following the Dodecanese campaign we have taken the story up to November 1943; in order to cover the range of SBS activities it is now necessary to return to an operation which took place in a different area the previous July. This concerned Langton's squadron, although Langton himself was not able to take part, being at the time in hospital. The effects of long periods of privation and discomfort had finally caught up with Langton. In order to speed his recovery he was posted back to Britain, where he joined himself to 1 SAS for the European campaign – a procedure which might in itself be described as a major health hazard.

Langton's squadron was taken over by Captain John Verney. (Verney, who later became a well-known author and painter, had been a contemporary of Jock Lewes in the same college at Oxford.) After the end of the battle in Africa (May 1943), the next step was Sicily, to be closely followed by Italy. Pantellaria surrendered on 11th June, so there was no need to pay any further attention to that island which had often been discussed as a possible target for raiding. Now the Higher Command felt that the SBS could be usefully employed in raiding airfields on Corsica and at the same time provide saboteurs for operations in front of the invasion forces in Sicily. The latter elements were to be provided by those members of L Squadron who were not required for Sardinia.

Verney was directed to command the Sardinian operation. The force was to be in two sections, the first under Verney to be parachuted in on July 7th; the second, commanded by Captain Brinkworth, on July 14th. The expedition had had a false start because the original plan had been to land by submarine and canoe. This method had been abandoned because after a few hours at sea the SBS party was feeling distinctly ill. Some of the illness was attributed to malaria, which had been plaguing them, but more of it seemed the effect of faults in the air-conditioning. Before they had gone very far the submarine developed engine trouble and had to return, and the SBS party were extremely happy to leave it.

The parachute drop went well apart from the fact that the ground was too hard for them to dig holes in which to bury their parachutes, and bushes, in which they endeavoured to hide them, were so scarce that the process took much longer than they had anticipated. They eventually located the airfield and liberally applied their bombs to suitable targets such as aircraft and fuel dumps, and cut all the telephone wires they encountered. They had no difficulty in avoiding sentries while doing this and only met one challenge as they left the airfield. Their challenger was reassured by Verney, whose command of the German language was just equal to the occasion: the sentry must have been badly shaken a few minutes later when the entire airfield seemed to be going up in flames.

Verney then set off in the direction of the coast. This was a difficult journey, for enemy patrols were now scouring the countryside in search of them. The local *carabinieri* were also active but less sure of themselves. When Verney's detachment ran out of food they calmly walked into the village shops and bought fresh supplies. Unfortunately they were unable to reach the coast where they would have been picked up, nor could they rendezvous with the rest of their party. Marching from point to point, occasionally being challenged by Italians whom they told they were Germans, or by Germans whom they told they were Italians, Verney's party lasted eleven days before they were finally captured. Brinkworth, who had been allotted an airfield which turned out to be unused, had remained at large for seventeen. His group's period of liberty would have been considerably less if they had not displayed such self-confidence that the Italian *carabinieri* and Sardinians whom they met could not believe, for a long time, that they were anything but what they claimed to be. By the time they were arrested the whole island was under the impression that the Allies had sent hundreds of parachutists, so often had Verney and Brinkworth and their parties been seen.

Successful though Verney's operation had been, their capture takes both him and Brinkworth out of this story. Although Verney escaped in Italy whilst the Germans were taking him to a prison camp in Germany, he did not return to the SBS. Like

Langton he joined the SAS and fought in North-west Europe until the end of the war.

The remainder of L detachment, who had been assigned to jump into Sicily accompanied by various members of 2 SAS, also had an interesting time. Their adventures were bizarre from the beginning. First, as they were flying towards their destination they had suddenly seen the green light, which was the signal to jump, appear rather unexpectedly. Assuming that the aircraft had reached the dropping zone (DZ) rather earlier than expected, they promptly jumped. Soon afterwards when the aircraft was over the DZ, the despatcher was mystified to find there was nothing for him to do as his parachutists had all gone already. The operation was code named 'Chestnut' and there were soon remarks about it being an old joke but not a good one. The party was in charge of Corporal Summers, who was nicknamed 'Safari' from his fondness for long endurance marches. Summers jumped with a pigeon tied to his chest; the pair of them landed among rocks but by some miracle were unhurt. In the area in which they had landed it was difficult to find enough military information to make up a message for the pigeon. They could find little to damage except telephone wires. Their supplies were limited as the containers which should have accompanied them had landed elsewhere. They were embarrassed to find that the local people insisted on treating them as liberators. When eventually they located targets they found these were extremely well guarded by alert soldiers.

Having done everything they could and having used up all their small stock of explosives, Summers and his party decided to return to the British lines which they knew would be somewhere to the south. Several times they were nearly captured by Germans; eventually they encountered a patrol of Seaforth Highlanders. The latter were not impressed by a party of scruffy-looking men appearing from the other side and were disposed to treat them as spies or something equally unwanted. The welcome Summers' party might have hoped for was definitely not forthcoming; until their *bona fides* were established at Battalion HQ they had the experience of being regarded with the utmost suspicion.

CHAPTER 6

Keeping up the Pressure

With the Aegean under German control the opportunities for the SBS seemed unlimited provided they could stay alive and uncaught; in the event it was not quite as easy as that, for other Allied organizations had their eyes on the Aegean too. SOE, for example, wished to establish bases at which information might be collected and future operations planned. People who wish to infiltrate quietly into an area and stay there unsuspected do not appreciate it if the island is then put into a high state of alert following a raid by SBS or a kindred organization. This is understandable enough, but proved very frustrating for the SBS who would be told that a cetain area was out of bounds and they must leave it alone; no explanation was given for this restriction, and it is now easy to see why this should be so. GHQ, with a dozen requests for priorities and with many long-term objectives in view, was certain to make decisions which were baffling to those they affected and might often be based on incomplete information. In spite of these minor impediments there was plenty to be done.

One of the first raids was on Simi. The garrison consisted of a mixed force commanded by a German major: he had eighteen Germans and some sixty Italians, as well as a force of *carabinieri*. The raiders, led by Lt Bury, decided to begin with the Commander's house. This had been damaged in an air raid and at first seemed deserted; it was a large building and much of it was still intact. When the SBS heard voices, they crept up to the window and threw a grenade inside among the occupants – German soldiers now converged on them to discover the origins of the disturbance. As they paused to organize the investigation, Sergeant Geary of the SBS caught them with a long burst from his Schmeisser. Schmeissers were machine-pistols which fired a magazine of 32 9 mm bullets at a rate of 500 r.p.m. The burst was enough for the Germans, who all fled. Another German now appeared at a window and was promptly shot by Bury. This seemed to be a satisfactory beginning, but in case the Germans might wish to use the building again he decided to demolish it. This was accomplished with 25 lbs of explosive and no doubt also accounted for any of the enemy still remaining in the building as well.

Lapraik, a short distance away, was also making good use of his time. He set fire to the caïques in a harbour, blew up a power station and demolished a food dump. These activities caused the Italians manning machine-guns around the harbour to open fire. Sgt Whittle sprayed each in turn with Bren fire, and the machine-guns ceased to operate.

Lapraik now began a tour of the islands, using two caïques. He put a patrol on Nisiros which blew up the telegraph station, destroyed the landing stage and also blew up all the caïques which were currently being used by the Germans. Then he moved on to Piscopi where there was little to destroy but on which he disarmed the *carabinieri*, to the amusement of the local population who resented the Italian presence.

He then returned to Simi where local information identified an enemy machine-gun post near the harbour for them. This they destroyed. An attempt was made by an Italian patrol to impede their departure but this was greeted by a swift burst of automatic fire.

This opening raid on Simi had a considerable effect on local morale. The Greeks welcomed it as a sign that the Allies would return and liberate them; the garrison reasoned much along the same lines and nineteen of them, including four Germans, deserted by rowing to Turkey to be interned there.

In hindsight it seems that there was excessive secrecy over the activites of special forces in this and other areas. All the men serving with the SBS were officially not in the Greek islands at all but with their original units. By this means it was thought that wives would be less worried than if they thought their husbands were engaged in hazardous operations and the Germans would be less able to detect how small were the forces operating against them. The Germans could scarcely be unaware that enemy forces were active in their area, but it might be marginally important to disguise their size. The type of person suitable for SBS and partisan operations is not given to talking about these either at the time or later. Years after the war the family of one such man was watching a television programme in which certain photographs appeared. 'That chap looks just like you, Dad,' they said. 'Yes,' said the father, 'you'd expect it to. It is me.' Having made this rash confession, he amplified it by explaining that while he was on that particular mission he had had to pretend to be on an anti-aircraft site in Alexandria. His letters, which consisted of little more than good wishes and enquiries about the well-being of those at home, were forgiven for their dullness because it was thought that his military life was one of unbroken routine and boredom: his family were happy to think he was having such a safe war. When, as sometimes happened, a man received a decoration, a suitable though untrue story had to be concocted for his family. The existence of the SBS was acknowledged but it was generally thought to be an organization for pleasure trips for those on leave.

Langton's detachment was now re-established and brought back into use although neither Langton nor Verney were available to command it. The vacancy was filled by a parachutist known to Jellicoe since pre-war days; the two had met again in Cos, just before it was lost to the Germans. The newcomer's name was Patterson. Patterson, like all those who survive in special forces, was a devotee of hard and imaginative training combined with ruthless selection. Kindness of heart and a willingness to forgive mistakes shows an admirable Christian spirit but is disastrous in selection for special forces. One man's weakness, suspected earlier but later proved, can cause the loss of the lives of many. (The SBS, and the SAS too, learnt the hard way.) The formula which was eventually adopted was to create a series of tests which a suitable man would be able to pass but which an unsuitable one would fail; by these it would become clear to the candidate that he could or could not reach the required standard, and if the latter he would drop out of his own accord. Although every effort would be made to explain that failure to reach such exacting standards was not a disgrace, few unsuccessful candidates could avoid feeling annoyed and resentful.

Patterson began his SBS career at Athlit where the unit was training. His exacting standards were immediately noted. Officers and men were accepted or failed with totally impartial efficiency. This made him unpopular with many at the time, but those who stayed agreed they could not wish to serve under a better commanding officer. Unhappily for Patterson his abilities at selection and training made him essential to the training centre at Athlit and therefore the powers that be were reluctant to move him, but his turn would come.

A turn was about to come for somebody else rather more quickly than it would come for Patterson. That person was General von Klemann, the Governor of Rhodes. Von Klemann pointed out to his superiors that, as Rhodes had been won so skilfully and was such an undoubted thorn in the flesh of the Allies, it would be folly not to ensure that it was retained; the price of retaining it would be reinforcements and these must be supplied. They were a brigade of mountain troops, an infantry division, a fleet of Junkers 52s and a number of small boats – the boats were for maintaining communication between the islands and for transferring troops to other areas when required. Von Klemann distrusted the Italians and told them all to take an oath of allegiance to Hitler; those who demurred were sent to camps where they would be unable to be disloyal. He was firm and fair, even though he showed no mercy to any raiders who fell into his hands. He began a policy of strengthening the garrisons on islands where he thought this would be appropriate, but soon had to change his dispositions because these did not fit in with SBS activities.

The SBS, whose value was now appreciated by the Higher Command as never before, was at last allotted the support they had been looking for for years. This involved a substantial fleet of caïques, launches and coastal craft commanded by the Navy but well-disguised as harmless fishing boats of the type which regularly plied their trade between the islands. Aircraft stationed on Cyprus were briefed in giving an unpleasant time to any German ships they found among the islands, and several submarines began the blockade of Heraklion (Crete), Piraeus (the seaport of Athens), and Porto Lago on Leros, as well as making life hazardous for German transports in general.

There then began an intense phase of military and naval tactics. The German plan was to defend the islands with the minimum number of troops and with this aim in mind there was a policy of switching reinforcements rapidly from one area to another if a threat developed. The British tactics were to create situations where the German commander had to send reinforcements to a threatened island or risk losing it. Once those reinforcements had taken up their new positions, the British aim was to see that they stayed there by destroying their shipping; needless to say there was considerable bluff and counter-bluff in these arrangements. Each threat had to be made to seem larger and more dangerous than it was; equally the Germans soon learnt from mistakes. As mentioned earlier the activities of the SBS and the Navy were made possible by the benevolence of Turkey's neutrality: both used Turkish territorial waters as unobtrusively as possible. The Germans were well aware of what was going on but did not wish to break off diplomatic relations with Turkey at that stage in the war, still less to find themselves in a military confrontation on yet another front. But in case the Germans changed their minds and decided to attack British craft in Turkish waters, the British used caïques and launches which were heavily camouflaged.

Lassen returned to Calchi, to which he now had a sentimental attachment. He had become fond of the island and its people, and had been pleased when he heard of the excellent resistance they had put up against their German conquerors. When he arrived this time he found that the Germans felt so secure about Calchi, nestling under the defences of Rhodes, that they had left a garrison of six Italians only. Lassen took the Italians prisoner and stored their arms on his launch. Just as he was considering his trip finished he heard the sound of an approaching boat. It turned out to be a launch from Rhodes, containing six Germans which had made an unexpected excursion from Rhodes so that, if anything was wrong, it would catch the Italian garrison napping. In the event it was the Germans who were caught napping. As they approached they were caught in a burst of machine-gun fire that must have been the last thing they expected. Having no idea of the strength of the opposition, and not wishing to be killed by a second burst, they surrendered. As these captured Germans were accustomed to making trips to the islands, they were a source of much valuable information on German and Italian strength and dispositions.

The next target was Stampalia, which lies to the west of the other Dodecanese islands, close to the Cyclades group. This party was commanded by Captain Anderson, and included George Barnes. Both were formidable swimmers and as they set out in January gales, which can be very fierce and unpredictable in these parts, it seemed likely that their abilities might be fully tested. They managed to arrive safely and pulled into a sheltered cove. Stampalia is eleven miles long and has a hilly interior. It also has a history in which violent conflict has not been unknown; once during a siege of its castle the defenders threw down hives of bees, which had been previously stirred to exasperation, among the attackers – the siege was promptly lifted. Anderson's first move was to win the confidence of the local people (he had interpreters with him), and from them he learnt where the garrison's strongpoints and supplies were situation. These included a Junkers seaplane and five caïques. Although the weather was appalling, members of the party succeeded in reaching the seaplane and attaching the necessary charges.

When the seaplane blew up, the garrison realized that there were intruders but were not sure how many and where they were. They opened fire without doing any damage. The SBS now moved to the caïques and laid their charges. This involved swimming in the icy water and was not enjoyable. When the charges went up, the garrison once more fired off a number of shots at random. Two other caïques were then discovered nearby and these two were blown up also. This effectively isolated the Germans on the island.

Simi was raided by a party commanded by Lt David Clark. They came quietly ashore and arrived undetected at the headquarters of the German garrison. Clark wished to take the occupants prisoner but when he suddenly appeared at the door (unwisely) and told them to surrender, their response was to fire at him. The shot missed him but knocked his gun out of his hands. Instead of rushing after him, the Germans stayed in the room, doubtless considering their next move and estimating the strength of the raid. They may have thought that the appearance of Clark was an attempt to lure them into an ambush. Surprised at not being followed, Clark and his party went round to the window and threw in grenades. This killed the occupants but created a general alarm. The psychological effects of the raid were even greater than the physical ones, for the experience of being raided when in such an apparently safe spot implied that the raiders were more dangerous than had been anticipated.

Patmos, which is the northernmost island of the Dodecanese, was selected as a target for a party commanded by Captain Bruce Mitford. It is a small island in three sections joined by isthmuses flanked by two islets. As Mitford had a small, well-disguised caïque, he decided to take a chance on sailing directly into the harbour where he found two caïques flying the German flag. He opened fire on one and sank it, then received the surrender of the crew of the other. He then blew up the latter. The Italian garrison which was meant to defend the island clearly had no enthusiasm for the task and disappeared. Mitford then went around destroying the cable and telephone stations. Just as he had finished another caïque entered the harbour. Mitford boarded it and explained to the Greek crew that they had fallen into Allied hands but all would be well with them if they co-operated. The caïque was bound for Leros and contained supplies for the German garrison there. The supplies included six cases of champagne, ten casks of Pilsner beer, thirty kegs of Samos wine, twenty-five radios, and a huge quantity of lavatory paper. This was too valuable a cargo to lose, so he put it into the care of one man, Marine Smith, with instructions to sail it to the base at Yedi Atala but, if intercepted, to sink it rather than let it be recaptured. Smith successfully completed the voyage with the cargo intact, but when Mitford himself arrived shortly afterwards he found that some of it had suffered from what might be described as natural wastage. Doubtless Mitford's colleagues had wished to drink his health in his absence.

A raid on Tilos, also commanded by Anderson, lasted for

several weeks. At the time of these events Tilos was called Piscopi, a name given to it by the Italians under the impression that it was an earlier name and in any case had a more Italian ring to it. The coastline is very rugged and full of little anchorages; the interior is hilly although it does not rise above 2,000 feet. Although the island is small there were ample opportunites for concealment, and as the local inhabitants were friendly to the British and resentful of the Italians, Anderson was able to do much as he liked. Having demolished most of the garrison supplies, Anderson decided to finish off by an attack on the Germans stationed on the island. A leading figure in these operations was the indomitable 'Safari' Summers, whom we encountered in Sicily – he was now a Sergeant. The Germans made a spirited response, but never located their elusive attackers in the darkness. Raiders of course have the advantage of surprise, and can stage diversionary attacks to draw fire in to uninhabited areas; however, if raiders come to close quarters, either by accident or design, there may be casualties on both sides. On this occasion the SBS were fortunate in not sustaining any losses. It was not possible to know how many Germans were killed or wounded but it was thought that it could not have been less than fifteen. The number may seem small, but it had been considered adequate for the defence of the island. Now the Germans had to reinforce the island or abandon it altogether.

A few weeks later the SBS returned to the island to see which decision the Germans had made. While finding this out, a more immediately interesting piece of information came to their attention. This was that two boats, heavily loaded with troops and replacements for stores on Cos, were expected to call at Nisyros, a small island close to Tilos. Patterson decided that this was a raid in which he should take part, and set off with a team of eight. At the time Nisyros had no German or Italian occupants, so Patterson had no problems in arranging an appropriate reception for the boats, which turned out to be lighters. It would not be easy, for the lighters contained at least twenty well-armed men with light machine-guns for their protection. Patterson watched the Germans arrive and dock. They unloaded a few stores and stretched their legs. They seemed in no hurry to leave, but Patterson had yet to decide what would be the best method of attacking a force of three times their number. While the Germans were on board they had a further advantage in the boats' own armament, which was considerably superior to anything Patterson could bring to bear. However, the visitors seemed to have plenty of time and indeed there was a moment of panic when they took a short sightseeing trip along the coast. Fortunately they dropped anchor again and the prey was still near the trap.

The reason for their dilatoriness became all too clear when Patterson received a message from an orphanage on the island that the Germans had said that all the children must be moved to Rhodes. Patterson felt distinctly cheerful when told that the Germans would be sending up a party to evacuate the orphanage that same afternoon. Immediately he got in touch with the Reverend Mother who, he understood, was appalled and distressed at this arbitrary and apparently inexplicable decision. He informed her that her only hope of saving her charges from this arbitrary deportation was to take them out of the orphanage and conceal them at a safe distance. Their luggage was to be left at the door.

The nuns and the children hastily departed; Patterson's men moved into the orphanage. The Germans had now decided it was safe to leave the boats and one party was amusing itself in the town while the other was marching up the road to the orphanage. Patterson had by this time met an Italian who heartily disliked Germans and was prepared to dress up as a priest. The 'priest' then welcomed the Germans and conducted them to the refectory where they could have a drink and take over the children. When the Germans were all inside the monastery, one of them became suspicious and turned round. Behind were Patterson and Lt Harden (another redoubtable performer). A brisk battle now ensued within the passages and rooms of the monastery. The SBS was outnumbered but was more experienced at this sort of *melée*. At one particularly hot stage, Patterson's gun jammed. He was grabbed as a hostage by a German. Rescue came from an unexpected quarter. With Patterson was an American, Lt-Cmdr Ramsaur, who had accompanied the expedition as an observer – he had plenty to observe on this trip! He had not expected to be involved personally, but he had a pistol and he now drew it very promptly and shot the German. With two dead and seven wounded the remainder either leapt throught the windows or accepted the offer to surrender. The ones who thought they had escaped through the windows ran straight onto the sentries Patterson had posted outside.

Patterson now turned his attention to the German boats. Surprisingly they did not seem to be in a state of alarm, although they must have heard some of the shots in the orphanage for they had sent two men to investigate. By the time Patterson had taken up a position on a hill just above the harbour and was planning to attend to the crew with Brens, the investigators reached the monastery, saw their dead comrades and rushed out shouting. Patterson heard the shout and swivelled the Bren in that direction. That was the end of the investigators but the alarm had now been given.

Down below, working their way towards the ships, was the second SBS group under Harden. They had hoped to arrive undetected but as the alarm was given they abandoned concealment and ran for the ships. The Germans on board leapt to their feet and tried to reach the machine-guns, but several quick bursts of fire from the Bren drove them away and under cover. Nevertheless they persevered in their efforts but as soon as they opened fire they found that Harden's party was near enough to start lobbing explosive charges amongst them. This convinced the Germans that further resistance was useless and they accepted the invitation to surrender. The wounded were then handed over to the nuns to be bandaged up, pending their removal later; the remainder, a total of seventeen, were put on a launch and despatched to Turkey. Patterson accompanied them. The launch was then sent back for the stores, which included considerable quantities of food and wine; it also took on the German wounded. This party was put in charge of Sgt Stephenson and was nearly home when it ran into another German force. This consisted of three lighters and a caïque. The meeting was unexpected by both sides. The British, seeing the first two lighters, assumed they were the two they had captured and moved up alongside. As soon as they had done so, they realized the lighters were different ones and were full of armed Germans. A third lighter and a caïque now came onto the scene. The Germans were slow to react because they had not expected to encounter anyone except Germans in those waters.

Stephenson was the first to realize what had happened. With two others he jumped on board the nearest lighter and began to spray the closely packed Germans with bullets from his Tommy gun. He cut a path to the Breda machine-gun with which the boat was equipped and turned it amidships. Meanwhile the caïque, realizing that the launch was British, turned a 3 inch gun on to it and opened up. One of the shells started a small fire so, assuming that the launch was alight and probably sinking, the Germans made no attempt to stop it getting away. By the time they realized the launch was not going to sink it was too late to do anything about it. But in the general confusion Stephenson and his companions had been left on the lighter, where they were still merrily blazing away with the Breda. They quickly ran out of ammunition, both for the Breda and for their Tommy gun, but not before they had accounted for twenty-six Germans, it was established later.

Having decided that the remaining Germans had too much to do to pay much attention to the three of them, they slipped overboard and struck out for Turkey. It was a mile away, but they made it. They avoided internment and found their way back to the SBS base.

The next raid, on Stampalia, was commanded by Lt John Lodwick. This captured two senior German naval officers and also successfully attacked a German billet which at the time had twelve occupants. The 'double bag' gave great pleasure to Lodwick as he had learnt from local intelligence that one of the German officers had only arrived that day and was going to dine with the other. The arrival of unexpected guests in the shape of SBS at their dinner party was such a surprise that the Germans offered no serious resistance.

Lt Gordon Clarke now followed approximately the route which Mitford had taken in the adventure described earlier. His party also visited the port of Skala on Patmos. Although there is a fortified monastery on Patmos – which is more like a castle than a monastery – the Italian garrison was in Skala town itself. They were pleased to surrender, preferring to be prisoners of the Allies to being at the disposal of their unpredictable German masters. The SBS liked garrisons to fight and flee rather than surrender, for if you are moving around unobtrusively as a small raiding party the one thing you do not need is the presence of a dozen prisoners. On occasions, the SBS simply disarmed prisoners and told them to disappear into the hills if the Germans returned, which they were certain to do.

Balsillie took another party to Tilos, this time accompanied by an American war correspondent named Donald Grant. Balsillie had voiced doubts when informed he must take this extra member of his party, thinking he might be a hindrance, if only because a war correspondent was a non-combatant. However Grant was full of martial ardour and assured everyone he would fight as strenuously as anyone. In the event – which was the ambush of a German patrol – the war correspondent's carbine jammed and he was unable to fire a shot. It may be mentioned, however, that even if his gun had been in working order it was unlikely that he would have fired it in time to take an effective part in the action. SBS training concentrated on very rapid reactions to crises and a very high rate of fire. Training and re-training might seem unnecessary to mature and experienced soldiers, but military skills will soon diminish if not kept up by constant practice. Many an old campaigner returning to base at the end of a successful foray has been irritated at being put on a training course which practises the skills he has just been employing, but the idea is eminently sound. On the retraining course the old soldier may become aware that he has lost a little of his sharp edge; he hopes no one else notices it.

Lodwick was now allotted a substantial target on Kalymnos. The capital, Pothia, is a port. In that port was a repair yard containing fourteen caïques: one of these, they noted, belonged to the Gestapo. They fixed their charges on the caïque unchallenged by sentries and, when they had retired to a suitable distance, observed the results of their labour.

But on Kalymnos it became obvious that the Germans were learning the best tactics to use against the SBS. The technique of aiming a single shot at a German billet and then opening up with the Bren when the inmates ran out to investigate, proved unproductive. Instead the inhabitants slipped quietly out at the rear and began to work their way as a patrol towards what they thought was the cause of the disturbance. Sometimes they appeared not to have noticed, or at least to be unperturbed when a bullet hit their front door, but then the calm would be broken as they emerged, firing as they came. If the raiders, imagining the billet to be empty, had come closer to investigate, this charge of mobile firepower could be somewhat disconcerting. Several times the raiders had to run for their lives, hampered by their heavy weapons and ammunition but not daring to jettison either.

The response to previous SBS activities on Nisyros was flattering but embarrassing. After the second raid the Germans had installed a garrison of 150 on the island. The fact was discovered by three SBS men who had the confidence of one of the local villagers. It seemed that the Germans had his confidence too, for when the SBS woke up the next day in a cave they had been asssured was safe from German interference they were surprised to see Germans coming towards it. Assuming the raiders were still asleep, the Germans were rather careless and noisy in their approach. Of the five Germans, four were killed when the raiders brought their weapons to bear, but the fourth escaped. Snatching up their clothes, the SBS then set off naked. Although they paused to dress, they soon realized that of the remaining 146 Germans on the island there was no one not employed in trying to find them. The normal method of arrival and departure from these raids was by naval launch. The Navy would select a rendezvous at a take-off point and then deliver their cargo of raiders. The naval launch then had to remain concealed, though alert for instant action and withdrawal. Kalymnos was patrolled by Germans so the Navy, not wishing to be caught at anchor, put out to sea and came back in at the appointed time. The return journey was not easy, for the Germans were now well aware of the methods employed. By the time the raiders reached the rendezvous the Germans had almost caught up with them; as a last desperate fling the Germans decided to try to sink the launch. They did not succeed, but the final stages of the evacuation were, to say the least, delicately poised.

Operations were now focussed on Calchi. In view of the spirited resistance they had made to the German takeover and the friendly relationship shown on Lassen's second visit, it seemed that Calchi, close to Rhodes though it was, could perhaps be used as a temporary base for other activities, notably against Rhodes or Scarpanto. A party of SBS, commanded by Captain Blyth and consisting of Sgt Miller and Private Evans, Jones and Rice, travelled by caïque commanded by Sub-Lieutenant Tuckey and manned by RN seamen.

The results of the reconnaissance seemed satisfactory; there was no German presence, and the caïque made ready to depart and to report. At that moment four well-armed German coastal craft appeared at the entrance to the creek in which the caïque was sheltering. There was a quick exchange of fire, then the caïque was asked to surrender. While it was arranging to do so the SBS party dropped quietly over the side and swam to the shore. Then they hid. The Germans searched for them vigorously and repeatedly, but without success. Their presence must have been known to the islanders, but they were not betrayed. In view of the fact that their presence had originally been transmitted to the Germans they felt themselves lucky, but subsequently decided that there could have been only one traitor, although one had certainly been enough.

When the hue and cry died down Blyth's party decided to get to Rhodes, from which it was thought that escape would be easier. They arranged with a fisherman to ferry them over but halfway across they had the misfortune to run into a German launch patrolling the coastal waters. After a cursory examination it seemed as if they were going to get away with it, but the German boat returned and fired a shot. Blyth then signalled his surrender, not wishing to cause the friendly fishermen to lose their boat.

Blyth was separated from the others and quickly transported to a prison camp in Germany, but of the fate of the others nothing is known. It is possible that they were shot by a local Nazi carrying out Hitler's orders to execute commandos, SAS and SBS, but the Aegean is a long way from Berlin. It would seem surprising that the commander of the raiders should merely be interned if the others, who included Navy personnel, were shot out of hand. Usually, even in cold-blooded ruthless execution, somebody is a witness or somebody tells the story later, but the fate of this party remains a total mystery.

Members of special forces are well aware of the fate which may await them if captured but consider that their expectation of life is as good as most people's in wartime, particularly those in the forefront of an infantry attack, on a bombing raid or in a submarine. A more cogent fear is that they might be wounded and have to be left behind. In such eventuality they would hope to be picked up by friendly people and be nursed back to health. However, not every peasant is likely to be friendly if he considers that helping a badly wounded man might get him into trouble for no reward. He might think it better to let the man die or be killed by wild animals, and then rob the corpse. Although there are many unpleasant possibilities if a raid goes wrong, nothing is gained by contemplating them until they happen.

CHAPTER 7

Widening the Range

Nowadays, when so many people are accustomed to enjoyable holidays in the Greek islands, it must seem that the SBS were exceptionally lucky to be fighting their part of the war there. The SBS would doubtless agree, but their reasons for doing so would be unusual. Service with the SBS was enjoyable and satisfying to those who liked adventure and were indifferent to danger and discomfort. The weather among the islands can be particularly unpleasant in winter and early spring, and the SBS were exposed to it at its best and worst. Eventually long periods of exposure with the minimum of medical care, erratic feeding, and the need to be in a state of constant alert, takes its toll on the hardiest. As the war continued the SBS found another factor was added to their normal strains – frustration. When they contemplated how much more could be done with greater resources there was a sense of total bewilderment at the short-sightedness of the Higher Command and their political masters.

As we have seen, the SBS raids were just sufficient to keep the Germans in a state of perpetual anxiety. That anxiety was demonstrated by the number of troops they felt they had to keep in Crete, Rhodes and other key areas. Those troops would have been valuable in Russia or France and useful in Italy, although in the latter the Germans seemed to be doing quite well with the number they had. What baffled the SBS and anyone else who cared to think of it was that the Allies did not make an effort to retake the islands. By 1943 we were masters of the Mediterranean and the situation had changed greatly from the days when the islands had been lost to the Germans. With the probable date of D Day at least nine months ahead, the use of a few aircraft, ships and landing craft in the

Mediterranean could not upset the great strategy but could well upset the Germans, as well as hearten our allies and give confidence to long-suffering Turkey. But it was not to be. Churchill, much though he longed for this to happen, dared not risk conducting it alone. This was not so much because of the enormous disaster that a failure would be, but because strategy had to be rigidly agreed at the top, and Roosevelt and the American Chiefs of Staff would not support the idea. Furthermore, there was active opposition to a Greek island campaign. American assault boats, first denied because it was said they were all needed in the Far East, were not sent to the Far East but instead back to America. All that Britain could possibly do in the circumstances was keep the Germans on their toes with SBS raids.

Periodically GHQ looked ahead. One day the campaign might move to an area which needed mountain troops. An agreeable institution which had been established in the Middle East was a ski school. It was thought that Special Forces should be trained in skiing – they might after all be used in Norway if ever we invaded that country – and the SBS as Special Forces had to take their turn. Attendance at the school was not universally popular, although some members were appreciative enough. The majority wondered why on earth it was that when they were skilled in raiding, but often prevented from doing as much of it as they would have liked, they should be taken off to learn a skill for which there was no immediate, or perhaps even long-term, use. But GHQ had decided they would take part and take part they did.

In 1944 the SBS were widening their range of activities. The Dodecanese was the most easterly group of islands in the Aegean; the Cyclades lie to the west and are thus much closer to Greece. Here the Germans had set up a number of radio stations to monitor Allied shipping and air movements. S Squadron (Sutherland's) was given the brief to eliminate these radio stations. Lassen was directed to Santorini. Santorini was the centre of a massive volcano which erupted thousands of years before, destroying the island and much else in the Mediterranean in the process. Rather appropriately, it now brews a highly potent wine. Gordon Clarke was allotted

Amorgos, the most easterly of the Cyclades, and also Ios, where Homer is alleged to have been buried. These were visited and the radio stations destroyed without difficulty. Mykonos, allotted to John Lodwick, is now famed as a popular tourist centre, although modern visitors will not fail to notice that the weather round the island can sometimes make a sea trip a memorable experience. The island is well populated and although Lodwick's party landed at night, apparently unseen and unknown, they found the next morning that their presence was well-known to the Greeks though fortunately not to the Germans. The raiders then attacked the German billet, in which seven Germans were known to be living. Two more were in the lighthouse.

The Germans in the billet put up a respectable resistance but, when informed that the building was about to be burnt down with petrol bombs, decided not to continue it. The two in the lighthouse were taken prisoners without a fight.

Lassen had found more resistance in Santorini than anyone had expected, but that pleased Lassen. The garrison, which was made up of forty-eight Italians and twenty Germans, had established its headquarters on the first floor of the Bank of Athens. Lassen, in one of his more thorough moods, was determined that no one should escape. Having previously blocked the exit, he went round the billet with his patrol at astonishing speed, throwing grenades into occupied rooms and spraying Bren bullets in all directions. The principal factor in Lassen's success was the speed at which he could move while still firing or lobbing grenades – In his earlier days he had been known to stalk stags and kill them with a knife. The fieldcraft, speed, and co-ordination which that required were now turned loose on the unfortunate Germans. Some, unwisely, tried to escape from the windows. It was said that of the original sixty-eight occupants only ten survived. That they survived at all was probably because Lassen thought they were already dead. Lassen was undoubtedly ruthless, but this was war. The SBS had two casualties: Casulli and Kingston were killed. The Germans gave them a full military funeral. The Germans were well aware that the SBS had been given good information about their dispositions, and demanded of the Greeks that they should give hostages. Six volunteered to take whatever form of brutality the Germans would mete out as a reprisal. The Germans shot them.

The war was becoming less chivalrous as the Germans felt the pressure mounting against them. On Ios the German garrison, when attacked by the SBS, used children to cover their withdrawal. This was not the first time in the war that children had been used to prevent the British achieving an objective. Earlier the parachutists who had blown up the Tragino aqueduct were captured by being surrounded first by Italian women and children and then by Italian soldiers. On Ios, Gordon Clarke made up for his inability to capture the garrison troops by capturing or killing others: he blew up all the telegraph and radio stations and destroyed dumps and caïques used by the Germans. He then moved on to Amorgos. Amorgos is a narrow island, eleven miles long with a population then of just over one thousand. At Amorgos he was joined by six members of the Greek Sacred Squadron. Although the SBS had great admiration for the prowess and courage of the Greek Sacred Squadron, their presence made them a little apprehensive for it was rumoured that the latter normally went into action expecting fifty per cent casualties and felt frustrated if they did not get them. The opposition would of course have suffered even more, but this type of head-on assault was not suitable for the SBS, who would have been wiped out long before if this type of casualty rate had been acceptable. There were only ten Germans on Amorgos but they put up a spirited fight. Their billet was surrounded during the night and sprayed with bullets. The Germans were then told that if they came out with their hands up their surrender would be accepted. They came out, but blazed away with their automatics as they did so. It was a brave but foolish gesture; the SBS were not novices at this game. Before the Germans had crossed the open space in front of the house, eight of them had been killed; the other two reached the trees and escaped.

One of the largest islands in the Cyclades is Paros, which is roughly in the centre of the group. It is sixty-four square miles in size and has a population of over 6000. Because of its importance the Germans had decided to build a new airstrip on

Paros. Sutherland despatched Lassen to the island to give it the benefit of his attention. Lassen found that the airstrip was too well guarded to be dealt with on this occasion, for the workmen were still on the site. However, various billets were surprised and raided. The arrival of the SBS party was so unexpected that the Germans assumed they were bandits.

Gordon Clarke also went into Naxos, which had a garrison of eighteen Germans; islands which had recently had a garrison of six or ten had now been reinforced to double or treble the number. The garrison billet was surrounded and attacked with Bren fire and grenades. All the enemy were either killed or wounded in the murderous little action which followed.

This is not a complete account of the raids, for some were on small islands and on a very limited scale. But the fact that every island had been proved to be vulnerable and that even caïques were stopped and boarded at sea (the Greeks being allowed to proceed, the Germans taken over or sunk) made the Germans give the area a high priority in defence. The Italian garrisons were less than whole-hearted in their tasks. Owing to a complicated set of treaties dating from the Italo-Turkish wars of 1911–12, the Dodecanese had been intermittently under Italian rule till 1922, after which the Italian suzerainty was continuous. The Greeks and Italians had developed a form of mutual tolerance although the Greeks had scant respect for Mussolini and his fascists. When Italy had attacked Greece in October 1940 and been repulsed, the Greek islanders had turned from tolerance of their overlords to contempt. Subsequently, when Italy had failed to conquer Greece and had been saved by her German ally, both Germans and Italians were regarded with active distaste.

When in September 1943 Italy made a separate peace with the Allies, only to find that the German response was to treat her former partner as a subject state, the future of the Greek islands seemed once more in a state of flux. As we saw, the Germans moved as quickly as they had in Italy and took control. But as we have also seen, that control with its attendant responsibilities became an increasing burden as a result of the activities of the SBS. The Dodecanese and Cyclades were well garrisoned and in a state of alert during

1944. The Greeks, who had had their territory invaded, were ready to be co-operative but had to be very wary of German ruthlessness. The Italians would have liked to see the Germans depart without further bloodshed, but could not visualize that happening, and while they were co-operating with the Germans they had to accept the same liabilities.

Sutherland's squadron was relieved in 1944 and its duties were taken over by Lapraik's. Lapraik was away temporarily when this happened and the squadron was under the command of Captain S. Macbeth. Macbeth made a reconnaissance of the Dodecanese and decided that the Germans were taking their defence very seriously. He looked for fresh fields to conquer and decided that these should be the Sporades, the most northerly group of islands in the Aegean. These at first appeared not to have attracted the German attention but he was informed by the inhabitants that the Germans had a garrison on Pelagos, an island to the east of the group. The enemy were said to be in a monastery. The SBS approached by night, surrounded it, and began to creep forward cautiously. There was a figure outside, presumably a monk, but the monk behaved in a very unmonklike way by hurling a grenade towards them. The grenade did not explode but even it it had the 'monk' might not have heard it, for as it left his hand the SBS opened fire.

There was a pause, both sides waiting for the other to make the next move. The SBS took the initiative and sprayed the surrounding vegetation with incendiary bullets. Thinking that the monastery might be the next target, the German occupants made a dash through the billowing smoke. There was a very swift, very brief, exchange of shots. The Germans then capitulated.

Raids of this type were the least of the SBS problems in the Sporades. A more menacing enemy was the weather. Those who might have wondered why it took Ulysses ten years to sail back from Troy to the island of Ithaca now began to feel he had made rather good time if he had experienced similar weather to theirs.

It was, however, clear that there would be no more 'soft' targets. This was shown very clearly when they paid a return visit to Kalymnos. This was now known to contain sixty Germans, so a substantial party was sent to deal with them. On this occasion the Greek Sacred Squadron formed the larger element of the party, with fifteen of their members, including Major Kasakopoulos who was put in overall command. The SBS element numbered ten. It was an interesting experiment to run a joint operation and it worked, though not without difficulties.

The attack was mounted on 1st July 1944; its objective was Vathi Bay, where the garrison was stationed. There was nothing subtle about the attack except that it took place at night; otherwise it was a normal three-pronged assault. The opening moves soon demonstrated all the fallibilities of night attacks: it is hard to tell which is the enemy and which your own side. Even in daylight it is easy enough for one patrol to fire on another if the action is confused; at night almost anything can happen.

The German reaction to the attack was to try to pinpoint opponents, so they sent up a sequence of Very lights which turned night into day. Realizing that their billets were being attacked, they brought down mortar fire on the surrounding area. This was followed by the arrival of German reinforcements. With the buildings now alight and a number of Germans killed it was clearly time to go. Unfortunately several of the SBS had been wounded. They were hidden overnight by a friendly Greek but the next day felt that there was no alternative but to give themselves up, which they did. They were not well treated, being mercilessly interrogated while still in great pain from their wounds; this was probably only to be expected. The Germans became very nervous after this raid. They believed that many more SBS men were probably still on the island and that this action was merely the prelude to a much larger incursion, probably a full-scale invasion. One of the three SBS prisoners died, but the other two escaped later. The Germans were right in guessing that bigger and more devastating raids were in store, but wrong in thinking that Kalymnos was the target – instead it was Simi, where Lapraik felt he had a score to settle. The main obstacle to any previous attack on Simi had been the presence of the Axis navy in the shape of four destroyers, but one of these was put out of action by a submarine, and another by the RAF. The remaining pair stayed quietly in Leros, waiting for the call of duty; clearly these also had to be put out of action before any large-scale operation could take place on Simi.

Somewhat surprisingly, and not entirely to the liking of the members of the SBS, a party of Royal Marine Boom Commando* Troops were summoned for the task. They had an up-to-date expertise in the very activity which had brought the SBS into being, but which had now become somewhat neglected as the SBS were now ferried round in naval launches or caïques. Boom commando troops are expert at getting to places where they are not wanted, and are made thoroughly unwelcome. They are as agile under the water as above it, sometimes more so. Their activities are very similar to those of naval frogmen but they specialize in entering guarded places. Placing a boom across a harbour and liberally blocking a channel with nets is no obstacle to those trained to circumvent such obstacles, as the Germans discovered on Leros. The main anchorage for Leros is Portolago, and here the destroyers were comfortably situated. After a Royal Marine visit with limpet bombs it seemed unlikely that those destroyers would ever leave Portolago again.

The Simi raiding party was on a much larger scale than anything before. It was 220 strong, eighty-one from the SBS, the remainder from the Greek Sacred Squadron. It was divided into three sections, each of which landed undetected. The main enemy positions were Simi castle and the monastery. There was fighting elsewhere but it did not last long. After a while the Germans in the monastery decided to evacuate it but did not succeed in getting away. The garrison of thirty-three was taken prisoner. In the other section 151 were taken prisoner. The SBS had six wounded, none killed; the Greek Sacred Squadron lost two; enemy losses totalled twenty-one. Wholesale demolition of installations then took place: these included gun emplacements, ammuniton and fuel dumps. and caïques to the number of nineteen. The prisoners were embarked on captured

* See Appendix II

German barges. Stellin was left behind with a rear party to slow down the inevitable German reoccupation of the island. This he did by opening fire on the two launches which came in as the spearhead.

This was the swan song for the SBS in the Aegean, for the Greek Sacred Squadron had now been sufficiently trained and organized to take over the area. The SBS was withdrawn as it was felt that its exploits could now be put to further use around Yugoslavia, Albania, and the Adriatic generally. A change is as good as a rest.

CHAPTER 8

Adriatic Adventures

In August 1944 the SBS set up its headquarters in Monte St Angelo on the Gargano peninsula on the eastern coast of Italy. From here they would attack suitable targets in Yugoslavia. Operations began with a swift raid on a railway bridge, destroyed by Lassen but not without detection and having to fight his way out. One of the problems in Yugoslavia, they discovered quickly, was whom to trust. One group which they obviously could not trust were the Ustachi, Croats who were supporting the Germans. The Ustachi were cordially disliked because it was said that their first action on taking prisoners – when they did – was to castrate them. Nowadays, when vasectomy is widely practised, it may be difficult to believe that members of the SBS would prefer being killed to being castrated.

After the German invasion of Yugoslavia in 1941 the Yugoslavs had seen little but trouble and disruption. Much of the latter was political. Germany and Italy had taken over Slovenia; the state of Croatia had been made up of the former areas of Bosnia-Herzegovinia and the district of Croatia, which was the centre of the Ustachi who were fascists and sympathized with the Nazis. Italy took over the Dalmatian coast and some of the islands off it and occupied Montenegro; Germany took Serbia and Banat.

There were other territorial changes in the area too, such as the Bulgarians occupying Eastern Macedonia. These all gave the new occupiers an excellent opportunity to pay off old scores or vent any suppressed hatreds on subject peoples who theoretically would not be able to retaliate. In Albania the fascists took advantage of the Italian rule to make themselves as unpleasant as possible to those who had previously disagreed with them – terror, murder and rape happened everywhere. This suited the Germans, because while the local inhabitants were directing their fury at each other they were unlikely to form a consolidated resistance to their conquerors. There were valuable strategic metals in Yugoslavia, such as bauxite from which aluminium is manufactured, and the Germans removed as much of this as they could as quickly as possible. However, there were two resistance movements in the country, both near the mountains where the majority of the minerals were situated. One was communist inspired and would eventually be led by Tito, the other was royalist and was led by Mihailovich. Mihailovich's followers were known as the Chetniks and were linked with the Yugoslav government in exile and the Special Operations Executive.

Tito began with 8000 adult supporters and a powerful youth movement backing it, but soon had so many victories that he attracted even more supporters and soon had 80,000 in the ranks. This dominated the countryside and made the Germans and Italians concentrate on preserving the larger towns and the most important communications.

Mihailovich had been equally active, but whereas Tito favoured a democratic republic Mihailovich wished to see the monarchy restored. Mihailovich felt that the future of Yugoslavia might be more assured if he reached an accommodation with the Germans. This obsession made him co-operate with them and actively oppose Tito; Tito went from strength to strength and by 1943 had founded the National Liberation Army.

But the Germans had relegated Yugoslavia to the background, not abandoned it. When the war in Africa was over and the Allies were forcing their way up the Italian mainland, Germany decided that it was time to reassert herself in Yugoslavia before the Allies made any advance there. The Germans conducted two punitive campaigns, the White and the Black, in which they brought the partisans to battle and inflicted heavy casualties: nearly two million Yugoslavs met their deaths through various causes in World War II.

But Tito's partisans were not beaten and Fitzroy Maclean, formerly of the SBS, who was now in Yugoslavia, was able to keep the British government informed of the turn of events. The British government was in a peculiar dilemma because although it wished to save the Yugoslav monarchy the movement's chief supporters had now gone over to full co-operation with the Germans. Tito's army continued to grow in strength and as this looked like being the only means by which the Germans would be ejected from the country the British decided that it must be given assistance, communist-dominated though it was. There was always a chance even at this stage that the Germans would mount an offensive and inflict a crippling defeat on the partisans who were very short of modern weaponry.

When the SBS were deployed against Albania and Yugoslavia the aim was to destroy as much German and Italian equipment as possible and help the local resistance. But, as we have already seen, some of the opposition was likely to come not merely from Germans but from collaborators such as the Ustachi and Chetniks. In view of the fact that penetration of Yugoslavia by boat was almost impracticable, most of the SBS were dropped by parachute; when these arrived they sometimes wondered whether they were among friends or enemies, so suspicious were their hosts.

A valuable operation was conducted by Lt Ambrose McGonigal, ably assisted by Lt Smith and Sgt Flavell and the rest of the patrol. This unit did in fact come in by sea and began by demolishing a railway tunnel. They were surprised to find that the principal opposition to their activities was provided by Chetniks. McGonigal then continued to pay attention to railway lines and ambushed several truck loads of German troops. Next he tried to capture a local German commander, but the information leaked and he was nearly captured himself. The difficulty with kidnapping operations was that you had to obtain knowledge of your victim's movements in advance. If your informant, having received your bribe, then decided to double his money he can proceed to do so by passing on your probable intentions not to mention your whereabouts to the enemy. On this occasion McGonigal avoided a trap and in return laid an ambush for the party of Germans which came to find him. The German party was caught in a valley and lost half its number of forty-five. The final move was the ambush of a troop train. This was affected by derailing the engine and opening up with machine-guns from each side of the track.

The effect of these raids on what the Germans had previously thought was an area completely under their control was demoralizing for its occupiers and heartening for the partisans. Nevertheless, when the Powers That Be decided that the SBS' talents were being wasted in Yugoslavia and would be better employed elsewhere there was no regret in the SBS.

The war appeared to be going very well for the Allies: The Germans were being pushed back by the Russian steamroller in the east and were also giving ground in Western Europe after the Normandy invasion. But the war was by no means over. London was still within rocket range; it would be optimistic to think that after producing the V1 and V2 rockets the Germans might not have an even more unpleasant V3 up their sleeves, and there was the underlying fear of the race for the atomic bomb. Apart from the possibilities of even more devastating weapons coming into use, the other uncertainties of war had to be reckoned with. Within a few months Germany would show, in the Ardennes, that she was by no means beaten. But with Tito's partisans virtually in control of Yugoslavia and with the Red Army approaching that country's eastern border, there was clearly little call for the SBS there.

A moment of truth may occur on two very different occasions for specialist troops. If a battle is being lost, specialist troops may be flung in as infantry, no matter whether they are signallers, parachutists, frogmen, glider pilots or anything else which has required a long and complicated training. Equally if a war is being won, and reaching the closing stages, a quick ending is needed and at that time specialist skills, once so valuable, are no longer required – all that is needed is for infantry to occupy and hold ground, but even at that late stage specialists can have their uses. Parachutists may be dropped ahead of advancing troops to seize installations which might otherwise fall into the wrong hands. When Japan surrendered in 1945 there was a delay before the Allies took over the areas which the Japanese had been forced to give up. In Malaya this gave the communists in the Anti Japanese Army the chance to raise their flag in the principal towns and proclaim that they had been liberated by the Communist People's Anti-British Army. In Indo-China the French did not get back before Japanese had handed over weapons to the communist forces of Ho-Chi-Minh, a delay which many would rue in years to come. And it was the same story in Indonesia. But not in Greece – the SBS were there.

CHAPTER 9

Greece

In the Autumn of 1944 Germany had decided to evacuate the southern part of Greece but not the north. The Germans wanted to make their evacuation in their own time and in a way likely to cause the maximum inconvenience to the Allies. They still had a network of garrisons and airfields in the Peloponnese peninsula, which is separated from the remainder of Greece by the Gulf of Corinth. Even the narrow neck of land (about ten miles wide) which joins the Peloponnese to the northern part is bisected by the Corinth Canal and the Germans could clearly see that their troops in the Peloponnese could easily be isolated. The more troops they had there, the greater the liability. On the other hand if they did not make a serious effort to keep control of the Peloponnese, that area would fall into Allied hands very easily and enable the latter to inflict punishing losses on the Germans still in the remainder of Greece. German reluctance to see the Pelopponese fall into Allied hands until the last possible moment was only matched by the fervent desire of the Allies to see that happen as early as it could be arranged.

The Allied plan of campaign was code-named 'Bucketforce'. It was commanded by Jellicoe, who had been promoted to Lt Colonel, and its aim was to seize the airfield at Araxos and begin operations from there. Araxos is in the north-west corner of the Peloponnese and is conveniently close to Patras.

In the event Araxos was captured surprisingly easily. Patterson, with fifty-eight under his command, dropped on to the airfield on 24th September. A previous reconnaissance had established that the airfield would only be lightly defended if at all, and in the event it turned out to have been evacuated already after heavy damage had been inflicted on the runways.

Patterson's squadron was reinforced by a further contingent of SBS who had landed at Katakolon, a nearby port. They then set off towards Patras.

Patras was a more difficult problem. There was one battalion of Germans there and two more of Greek collaborators whose activities were camouflaged under the bland title of security battalion. Patterson, knowing his numbers were under sixty, decided on a psychological approach. He deployed the squadron with great mobility and rapidity around the town, giving the impression that large numbers of troops were taking up battle positions, firing a few range-finding shots and then digging in. The facts were quite different. Having loosed off a few mortars the SBS then hastily departed to the next chosen site and repeated the performance. Patterson then contacted the head of the Red Cross, a Swede, and told him that he wished to avoid the bloodshed which would be inevitable if they had to make a full scale attack on the town. Civilians, he pointed out, would be the innocent sufferers. Through the Swede he managed to make contact with the German commander. The German commander may or may not have swallowed Patterson's story, but he knew that if he surrendered the town without higher authority he himself would be in serious trouble. Equally, even if Patterson's story was untrue at the moment, large Allied forces were probably in the vicinity and a heavy assault upon the town must be expected. He stalled by saying he would need permission from higher authority, which meant the German HQ in Athens. Patterson, feeling this was not a satisfactory development, tried to browbeat him but the German remained firm. In order to help the German commander make up his mind the SBS redoubled their mortaring of the positions of the Germans and the security battalion.

Jellicoe now decided that the security battalion was the next target. He employed an officer from SOE, who had been conducting clandestine operations in the area for the past year, to make contact with the security battalion and leave them in no doubt about the danger of their positions. The security battalion knew very well what could happen to them once their German protectors left; at best they would be shot by the partisans whom they had been trying to track down; at worst their fate would be lengthier and even less pleasant. Their best policy, Jellicoe pointed out, would be to surrender to him. He gave them a short time to think it over, and that was all the time they needed; 1600 promptly surrendered. It was a success but a problem too. All Jellicoe could do was to isolate them, arrange for their food, and make the partisans promise not to molest them. Miraculously the promise held.

The complicated affairs of Greece now need a brief explanation if the next phase of SBS activities is to be understood. When Greece had been conquered in 1941 a number of independent resistance groups were promptly formed. Unfortunately they hated each other as much as they did the enemy. This, regrettably, is often the case with resistance groups who sometimes will actually impede their fellows. This was as true in Greece as anywhere else, and applied strongly to Crete. In order to substitute co-operation for rivalry, SOE sent a team of skilled negotiators and Grecophiles to parachute into Greece in October 1942. A similar team, with the same aim in mind, went to Crete.

In Greece the principal resistance movements were the National Liberation Front (EAM) which had a communist dominated army known by the initials ELAS, and the EDES, which was composed of moderates and royalists. Not surprisingly, they hated each other, but the SOE mission mentioned above, led by General E. C. W. Myers and Colonel C. M. Woodhouse, persuaded them to forget their differences in the common cause of liberating Greece. Their efforts were rewarded when the two groups co-operated to blow up a viaduct on the railway between Salonika and Athens. This occurred just before the Alamein battle of October 1942, and doubtless had a considerable effect on it, as eighty per cent of German supplies to North Africa were said to travel this way.

The co-operation was fragile; although for a year the two groups worked well together, the progress of the Allies in Italy made them aware that before long Greece too would be liberated. When that time came each group wished to hold the reins of power and they therefore began making preparations. EDES remained loyal to the British, feeling that this offered their best chance, but ELAS was clearly more interested in its own political aims and returned to its former hostility to EDES. Britain promptly cut off its supply of arms to ELAS; ELAS then saw the error of its ways and agreed to co-operate once more. A joint command for resistance organizations was appointed, to be called the Provisional Committee for National Liberation. The king in exile, George II, brought into his government George Papandreou (at the time of writing in 1983 Prime Minister of Greece once more) in the hope that he could reconcile the hostile factors. This was the situation when the SBS arrived in Patras.

In spite of their success with the security battalion the SBS had by no means won the town. A task force from Italy was said to be on its way but unless it arrived soon the SBS would be counter-attacked, or worse, the Germans would evacuate having destroyed everything likely to be useful to the Allies. The most vital area to be saved from this fate was the port. The SBS took the high ground overlooking the port and turned a captured German gun on the Germans who were making their way in – these retreated and left the area clear for the SBS who then had the delicate task of removing demolition charges. This success made possible the entry of the task force from Italy, and Jellicoe, Patterson and co. were able to leave others to sort out the chaos left in the evacuated city where many old scores were being settled. The SBS bluff combined with German uncertainty had captured a major town with minimal bloodshed.

The next move was to reach Corinth as quickly as possible and cut off any Germans still remaining in the Peloponnese. 'As quickly as possible' turned out to be not as fast as they would have liked, for the retreating Germans had used explosives to make the road less usable than it had been for themselves. Corinth was reached on 9th October. The RAF was very active over the retreating Germans, and the EDES guerrillas were also harassing them. ELAS were noticeably absent from these operations although they could very well have interrupted the retreating columns. The reason was simple enough: the Germans had handed over arms to ELAS in return for an unmolested passage. The Germans demolished the pontoons on which they crossed the Corinth Canal, thereby temporarily checking the pursuit, but Patterson found a nearby ferry which was still undamaged and the SBS were across.

Contact with the Germans was established again at Megara and an attempt was made to cut them off by ambushing the rearguard. Balsillie took a caïque to reconnoitre the Bay of Salamis when he landed and entered Piraeus, but the Germans were too numerous to be stopped. Meanwhile the 2nd British Parachute Brigade was dropping on to Athens airport. SBS activities were now directed to preventing an orderly evacuation from that city. They were provided with reinforcements from 4th Independent Parachute Brigade, but these had the unfortunate experience of being dropped in gale force winds and losing one third of their number. Nevertheless the sight of British parachutists floating out of the skies to land behind them had a quickening effect on the Germans resolve to evacuate. Those on Megara slipped away. Jellicoe was sent to Athens to report on conditions in the city which seemed likely to be turbulent in view of EAM/ELAS antagonism. Jellicoe and Milner-Barry set off in a caïque accompanied by Patterson and most of his squadron. They reached Scaramanga but then found themselves without transport: the Germans had taken everything except two bicycles. Jellicoe and Patterson took one each and bicycled into Athens. It was not the way conquering heroes enter cities, being less impressive than elephants, tanks, warhorses or even jeeps, but it did very well. The SBS, and particularly their commander, had a detestation of publicity and ostentation, and the liberation of the centre of ancient democracy by two men riding that most democratic of conveyances, the bicycle, was very appropriate.

It did not take Jellicoe long to size up the situation in Athens – trouble brewing. Both EDES and ELAS were present in force and in no mood to compromise. Meanwhile there was more important work to be done before these local issues could be settled, although the SBS had not yet seen the last of Athens. Soon they would be needed there again.

In most countries where there was resistance to the Germans the hard core had come from the communists, and it was the communist-led forces which had given the Germans and Italians the most trouble. In Greece, this was not so. ELAS, the communist-dominated resistance group, made various deals with the Germans, usually for arms; when they received these arms they turned them against rival resistance groups, and even against their liberators the British. Eventually Britain had to transfer two divisions from the Italian front to quieten the trouble when ELAS captured parts of Athens and Piraeus. The fanaticism of politics knows no limits. It is interesting to recall the arguments for making an Allied drive up through the Aegean a year before. Had that occurred, ELAS would have had no chance to make separate deals with the Germans, and Greece would have avoided much post-war turmoil.

Meanwhile the SBS pressed on. The going was slow as the retreating Germans had done their best to make the road impassable, and with German thoroughness they had almost succeeded. The SBS had now departed a long way from its usual methods of attack. It now had under the command of Patterson members of the RAF regiment which had given a helping hand at Patras, some field guns manned by the Royal Artillery, and a parachute battalion which was being used as conventional infantry. This column moved up through Larissa and Elasson to Kazani in the centre of northern Greece. Here the Germans decided to make a stand. They had with them a security battalion. This was offered surrender terms by Patterson, but the security battalion refused the offer, not uninfluenced by the Germans.

The attack went in the next morning. The Paras did very well on the right flank and captured the central high point; they were lucky to have got away with fifteen casualties. The SBS had a harder time as they were observed as they approached and caught on open ground. They fell back and brought their mortars into action. The advance continued. The second obstacle was a strongly-held German position, a building used as a barracks. For this the field guns were employed but the Germans replied and the action seemed to have settled down into an artillery exchange.

Suddenly the pattern was broken. Once more the Germans were withdrawing. Patterson's force kept as close to them as they could, but eventually contact was lost. The SBS paused, regrouped, took stock, and went on again.

The next engagement took place on the Yugoslav border. Here the SBS was just able to outflank the German column as it passed through a narrow valley. There was a short and very bloody action, with the Germans at a disadvantage. Eventually the Germans forced their way through into Yugoslavia, which was forbidden territory for British troops.

Meanwhile Sutherland's squadron was active in Albania, and Lassen was visiting the islands off the Greek coast to discover if there were any German positions there. But in October Lassen was recalled to the Sporades. He took forty men to flush out the few Germans left on the islands. Scopolos and Volos had both been abandoned. At one point the troops found themselves caught up in Greek politics, for as they approached a bay in Volos they were fired upon by the EAM. The EAM had mistaken them for ELAS. This would have been funny but for the fact that Lt Bob Bury was shot, and died quickly.

Lassen was now directed to Salonika, which the Germans had not yet evacuated. He took his caïque up the Potidhia canal and surveyed the scene through binoculars: he then took a closer look from a jeep and found the Germans had just left and ELAS was in charge. Enquiries about the direction the Germans had taken were met with sullen uncooperativeness. Lassen continued his reconnaissance and found that the Germans had abandoned Salonika itself but were still demolishing their dumps on the outskirts. Lassen decided this must stop. He acquired four fire engines and loaded his squadron on board. With these he was able to rush up to the Germans and catch them unawares. The fact that the Germans were retreating and blowing up petrol and other dumps did not seem to Lassen any reason for supposing that they were any less at war now than at any time previously; in fact the war would not be over for another six months. Lassen and his men went in with guns blazing. The German demolition party, numbering about sixty, was simply wiped out. It was thought by some that Lassen should have asked for their surrender and risked losing some men if they demurred – that was not Lassen's way. Later he may have changed his mind, but not yet.

Lassen's actions in Salonika were subsequently thought to have been well justified. His small party was so mobile, so warlike, and covered so much ground that its sighting was reported all round the town. The townspeople, and particularly ELAS, gained the impression that the British were there in at least battalion strength. This had a calming effect on those who sympathized with ELAS and also on those who might otherwise have thought this was appropriate moment to pay off old scores.

Elsewhere around the Aegean, Lapraik was visiting former haunts. Crete, Cos and Simi were among them, but Rhodes and Crete remained occupied. In Crete the German garrison had been reduced as much as possible to supplement needs elsewhere. The original numbers had been close to 100,000 but were now down to not much more than a thousand. Those remaining were constantly harassed by partisans ably assisted by members of Force 133 who were SOE specialists on Greek problems. The island was blockaded but its final surrender was left to the organization of the SBS. Lassen, once more, was told to renew his acquaintance with Crete.

The Germans had wisely decided not to try to hold the entire island but to concentrate on the north-west corner which contained Maleme airfield. There were still plenty of them and they were not likely to give up without a fight.

Lassen arrived on 3rd December and based his squadron at Heraklion. His patrols combed the evacuated areas carefully for German stay-behind parties. Lassen was aware that they might be opposed by more than Germans, for ELAS had strong support in Crete and there were several other political organizations, varying from the extreme left to the extreme right, who wished to control Crete's destiny after the Germans left; the presence of the British was not therefore entirely to the liking of the local political leaders.

There was a blockade on the sea side of the German-held part of the island, and the inland perimeter was also theoretically sealed. The people responsible for the latter were the Andartes, a body of Greek auxiliaries. The land blockade was notably ineffective as the Andartes, though excellent in combat, seemed to be making a small fortune by breaking it and trading with the Germans. They were not over-pleased by the arrival of the SBS, who insisted they should be coopted into the next operation – a night attack. Lassen developed an incurable distrust of all Greek political groups on Crete when an ELAS supporter fired on a jeep, killing an SBS officer, but soon afterwards SBS duties were taken over by other formations and Lassen said goodbye to Crete for the last time.

The SBS came back to Athens at the end of 1944. ELAS had suddenly called for a national insurrection to take over power. The Allies had no intention of allowing this to happen, and the SBS were therefore among those drafted in to prevent it. It took a month before order was restored and it was a month of much tedium, occasional street-fighting and some losses. The SBS had more casualties in Athens than in many more worthwhile assignments: three of their members were killed and twelve wounded. It was the unwholesome type of warfare to which many soldiers would become accustomed in post-war days. The enemy rarely wore a uniform, often responded to friendly gestures with treacherous attack, and knew no rules of war.

Jellicoe left the SBS for higher things in December 1944 and his place as commander was taken by David Sutherland. The SBS took a severe blow at this time when Ian Patterson was killed in a Dakota crash near Brindisi. The aircraft was carrying wounded to hospital when something which was never explained went wrong with the controls; there was only one survivor.

Sutherland's first assignment was to attack those Adriatic islands which the Germans still held. For this his base would be Zara, a former Italian town which had been cleared of Germans but was now in the hands of Yugoslavians who managed to be obstructive and condescending at the same time. Most of the Italians who would normally have been in Zara had been dispossessed. On this, as on other occasions, Allied troops would have found it easier to deal with their former enemies than with the uncooperative friends their efforts had helped to liberate.

The German-held islands were not likely to be an easy assignment: they were garrisoned by experienced and determined soldiers. Although there was a general impression in the world that as the Russians were approaching Germany from the east and the Allied forces were approaching from the west the Germans would not wish to protract matters indefinitely, this unfortunately proved to be far removed from reality. The more it became clear to the Germans that they were losing the war, the more fanatically determined they became to raise the price of victory as high as they could. In the Adriatic islands there were many who had previously been in the Aegean, and these knew what sort of raids to expect and what were the best methods to combat them; they spent their time by endeavouring to make their positions impregnable with barbed wire and well-concealed mines which had reached a very sophisticated state. Often they were booby-trapped against dismantling, and some were sown in pairs so that as the top one was lifted off the bottom one would explode. Every form of fiendish ingenuity had been exercised in the design and manufacture of mines. Apart from mines on land, there were large numbers in the sea. Doubtless the position of all these had been marked when they were first laid, but since then many of the original charts had been lost even before the minelayers had left for other areas. Furthermore, some mines had broken away and were drifting freely. The Adriatic Sea had become distinctly unsafe for navigation.

An early raid was on Lussin where there was a German strongpoint. The raiders were commanded by Captain McGonigal and included Lt Thomason and Lt Jones-Parry. As they approached they were observed and fired on, so as surprise had been lost there was no alternative to the full-scale attack which McGonigal now ordered. As there were forty-five Germans in the strongpoint this was going to be no easy task. The SBS reached the building and started to work from room to room. This was a delicate operation for it was a night raid, the lights had been put out, and no one knew exactly where the enemy was. The SBS had several casualties, one being the newly-joined Lt Parry-Jones. He was hit by a burst of automatic fire. As he was still able to walk, a field dressing was put on his wounds and he was told to make his way back. It was two miles to where the boat was waiting. On arrival he was asked how he felt and he admitted he did not feel too good. Subsequent examination showed that he had walked the two miles with a shattered right arm and a bullet in his spleen.

A raid on Cherso was more successful and less costly: twelve of the enemy were taken prisoner. A useful gain here was the capture of the enemy radio code books. Radio code books give the code names of all the units in the area. The capture of them has several valuable effects: it gives you a list of all military, air, and naval forces in the area; it can be used to transmit false information; it can be used to persuade the enemy they are communicating with their friends rather than their enemies; and lastly, when the loss of code books to the enemy is known, all codes have to be changed. Usually a unit will have code books which can replace the captured ones, but if codes are lost often enough it is possible that certain units will run out of code replacements. In any event there is always a chance that a few units will not realize the codes have been changed and will keep on transmitting under the old codes, which can cause remarkable confusion.

The next move was an attempt to destroy the bridge linking the islands of Cherso and Lussin. This was assigned to McGonigal with thirty-eight others. The bridge had been bombed many times without success. It was defended by a German garrison of eighty men, well-armed with a variety of weapons including anti-aircraft guns.

The attack went in on 18th March 1945 with two launches and one folboat: the folboat was manned by Sgt Holmes and Rifleman Lecomber. The raiders passed undetected when they immobilized a gun site, but they ran into a German patrol as they approached the jetty. The SBS opened fire first and with the advantage of surprise killed four of the Germans without loss to themselves. The remaining members of the patrol fled into the darkness, and the alarm had now been raised.

The bridge was surrounded by layers of wire, on which machine-guns were zeroed, and high walls. Speed was now vital, but when Lt Henshaw, veteran of many a battle, tried to cut the wire he was caught by a grenade and killed. A ding-dong battle now ensued with the SBS trying to approach the position as the Germans laid down a belt of machine-gun fire in front of it.

Clearly this stalemate could not continue or the SBS, who had now lost four men, would gradually be eliminated.

McGonigal sent a message to the launches to open up with their Oerlikons* – these gave the Germans an unpleasant time but failed to move them. Reluctantly McGonigal decided that the bridge was not going to be destroyed on this occasion. The SBS continued the attack until dawn approached, then disengaged. In some ways they were paying the penalty for their earlier successes. If a few highly trained men are able to inflict damaging losses on enemy installations which are insufficiently guarded, then presumably rather more of those same highly trained men should be able to demolish better guarded and larger targets but the reasoning is parallel to that which suggests that if a sword can kill a man, two swords should be able to fell an oak tree. Given time this might be true, but swords are somewhat wasted when an axe or saw would do the job better. The axe or saw in this case should have been a determined naval bombardment or air strike, but the target was not thought to be important enough to warrant it.

So the frontal attack had failed, but the bridge still remained as an important enemy asset. The remedy was to be more devious: if the bridge could not be destroyed, the approaches must be made unusable; that was more of an SBS task, so a series of ambushes was mounted and several vehicles including a staff car were attacked.

The tide of Allied victory was now gradually working its way up the Adriatic. The Italians in the garrisons began to desert; air attacks on German positions became more frequent. The final blow came when the Yugoslavs captured Ogulin, on the way to Fiume. The German-held islands now lay off a mainland which was in Allied hands: they could therefore be left as long as wished before their inevitable surrender. There was not a lot left for the SBS to do, except in Istria.

Istria has the sort of history which most border states have; it would be too much to say 'enjoy'. It is a peninsula which incorporates the important towns of Trieste, Fiume and Pola. After World War I it was taken from Austria and awarded to Italy, much to the disgust of the Croats and Slovenes. Fiume has now been renamed Rijeda. Changes of name or even of overlordship

---

* 20mm, fast-firing anti-aircraft guns, used on land and sea

do not usually alter the character of an area greatly, and so it was in Istria. The Istrians are sturdy, individually-minded, brave people; when recruited into the Italian army they had formed one of its better fighting units. The Istrians disliked all their masters and would-be masters with equal impartiality and intensity. There was a good chance that they might be prevailed upon to support the Allied cause, and for this purpose Sutherland sent Captain D. Riddiford to win their hearts and minds. Riddiford was pleased to find the Long Range Desert Group already operating there; though far from their original haunts they had adapted their technique to logging every ship which used those waters and recommending suitable targets to the Royal Air Force. He was less satisfied with a division of Yugoslav partisans who appeared to be doing nothing but pleasing themselves.

An SBS party commanded by McGonigal was despatched on 12th April 1945. It landed close to Fionona but not without problems, for there were many German boats in the area. If the Germans knew how badly the war was going for Germany, they showed very little sign of it; they also had a scorn for the partisans. The SBS soon developed an even stronger emotion for the partisans, for the local commander, looking not unlike the bandit which he had probably once been and might be again, told them they had no right to be in Istria and must therefore be disarmed and interned. The SBS brushed this aside but revised their sphere of operations so as not to clash too obviously with their alleged allies. The reason for this absurd posture by the partisans was that Tito's aim was to liberate Istria from the Germans and Italians with Yugoslav soldiers, and thereby make a convincing political show of power; the drawback to the plan was that the partisans in the area were particularly supine and inept. The best that could be hoped for was that the Germans would gradually withdraw, and that the vacated positions would then be occupied by partisans who would claim to have liberated them. That process might take some time, but time was no problem to the partisans. Apart from anything else, spectacular successes by British troops would reveal somewhat cruelly how unadventurous the partisans had been. The partisans therefore aimed to put every possible obstacle in the way of the SBS.

Sutherland, who had long had ambitions to operate in Istria where great damage could have been done to the Germans at an earlier stage in the war, was now forced to bow to political expediency. The partisans could do nothing about the Germans, but by complaining about the presence of the SBS they could and did impede the latter, who were ordered not to upset them. In consequence the SBS were left kicking their heels in Istria until Allied armies entered Trieste, after Tito had captured it from the western side. How right was Clausewitz when he said that war is politics carried on by other means.

The last SBS operation in this area was one of the strangest and saddest. The Italian campaign was now drawing to its close, but this long and gruelling grind was not going to end quickly or easily. There were few parts of Italy where an advancing army could not be checked by well-positioned defenders, and the Germans had undoubtedly used every natural feature to the best advantage. Positions like the Gothic line and the mountainous country north of it had cost thousands of British casualties. The winter of 1944–5 had been exceptionally cold and wet, turning small streams into rivers. The Eighth Army forced its way up to the Po delta and were hard pushed to hold their position. Ammunition was short; most guns were rationed to an average of twenty rounds a day. Both sides, in view of the needs of other fronts, had withdrawn troops from Italy. When spring 1945 arrived fine weather came with it, and Allied air supremacy was able to wreck most of the German lines of communication. The final Allied offensive was launched in April. The British Eighth Army went forward on 9th April and achieved marked success; on the 14th the American 5th Army also swung into attack. On 21st April Bologna was occupied, Verona fell on the 26th and on 2nd May the Germans surrendered. Their defence of Italy had cost them half a million casualties; the Allies had lost 312,000. The campaign had lasted nearly two years.

One of those Allied casualties was Anders Lassen. After the conclusion of the campaign further south, Lassen's squadron had been posted to Eighth Army. He was put under the command of Brigadier Tod who had a mixed brigade consisting of Commandos and attached forces. By temperament and experience Lassen was not an easy man to command, but he respected Tod and the feeling was mutual.

Tod was on the extreme right flank of the Allied line, and his own right flank came up to the edge of Lake Comachio, some twenty miles north of Ravenna. Lake Comachio is less of a lake than a flooded marsh, most of it about two feet deep but with deeper channels in some places. The 'lake' area is approximately twenty miles by sixteen, and between it and the sea lay a line of dunes which the Germans had fortified heavily as well as islands in the lake which the Germans had not neglected to fortify. The Germans were well aware of the vital tactical value of the area and had troops on the northern, eastern and western shores. Tod intended to establish a bridgehead on the western side and work forward to take the Germans in the rear; this outflanking move would jeopardize the German defensive plan and be of great benefit to the Allies. For Tod to carry out his operation successfully, Lassen and the SBS would need to make a diversion.

For the first part of his time in the area Lassen made a thorough reconnaissance of the lake. Needless to say this had to be done at night, often close to German-held islands. Lassen even once ventured up into the town of Comachio itself. Comachio is rather like Venice, with some waterways instead of streets. Here he was nearly captured by Mongolians who had been taken prisoner when the Germans invaded Russia. Some of these Russian prisoners had been forced to work for the Germans; others had decided to do so voluntarily. Lassen was lucky: two Italian fishermen decided to help him get away and went with him themselves. Lassen was very happy in this work, in which he was using folboats and taking personal risks. His right-hand man as always was Guardsman O'Reilly.

The attack took place on the night of 9th April, the night when the whole Eighth Army moved forward. The Commandos advanced, using the route Lassen had found to be feasible. Lassen and his patrol created the necessary diversion by landing on the northern shore near Comachio town. It was, of course, a somewhat suicidal mission. The aim was to create the impression that this was a large attack which was beginning quietly. Lassen's squadron was divided into three patrols. One, under Lt Stellin, was to land a few yards further along a few minutes later. Lassen disembarked very quietly and advanced down the road to the town. He was challenged near the first pillbox. The answer did not satisfy the Germans, who were very much on the alert. They opened fire, and this was a signal for several other pillboxes to begin sweeping the road with waves of bullets. It was a quicker and larger response than the SBS had expected, but it certainly suggested that the defenders thought that this was a large-scale attack which they must repulse at all costs. Unfortunately for the SBS there was hardly any cover here; when caught on a tarmac road and pinned down by a hail of bullets one can make an effort to press oneself into the surface, but this is not usually a very successful process.

Lassen quickly realized that so great was the volume of fire now sweeping the road (it was thought there were at least six machine-guns) that it could only be a matter of time before the entire SBS party was killed or wounded. He himself stood up, ran forward and lobbed two grenades into the first German pill-box. With this out of action he barely paused before going on to do the same to the next. This counter-attack caused the others to cease fire temporarily while they established which was friend and which was foe. During this unexpected lull Lassen darted back to the squadron and told them to follow him. They investigated the two pill-boxes which Lassen had attended to, and found two survivors. Both were Russians. These were escorted back to the boats. Very lights were now being fired from the German position, and the Germans began to rake the road with machine-gun fire once more. All this happened more rapidly than it can be recounted – Lassen had been told to create a diversion and he was certainly doing that. Stellin, who had intended to land unnoticed, now had no hope of doing so. On shore Lassen's patrols were in the middle of another brisk battle with bursts of Spandau and Schmeisser, the thump of grenades and the weird illumination of Very lights making it seem like a scene from *Dante's Inferno*. Lassen was totally indifferent to danger. He stood up, lobbing grenades, then ran forward spraying bullets around him. Using the first two pill-boxes as cover, he crawled forward to the third, stood up and threw more grenades. From inside the pill-box a German called out 'Kamerad'. Lassen paused, walked up to the entrance and spoke in German. He told the occupants to come out and surrender. Instead they replied with a burst of fire. As he fell he lobbed a grenade into the post. Sergeant-Major Stephenson, another faithful companion, dashed up. Lassen could still speak, though with difficulty. 'Steve, I'm wounded. I'm going to die. Get the others out.' A few minutes later he was dead.

With the order to withdraw, Stephenson had got the remainder of the patrol away. The diversion had been a success: the next day the Germans withdrew and regrouped.

Lassen was twenty-five when he was killed. Other members of the SBS swore that he had done more than anyone else to ensure its success; he would have denied this scornfully. His comrades cannot understand how he fell for the treacherous ploy which killed him, but perhaps he felt that to take a pill-box intact with hostages would have enabled him to establish a bridgehead and get the squadron out of what had undoubtedly become a death trap. In the mixture of dark, brilliant flashes of light, bursts of gunfire, screams, shouts, and the thud of grenades, a man might make a decision he would not have made in retrospect. Unfortunately for Lassen there was no retrospect. Few soldiers have been so greatly admired by their men. In his career he had been awarded the Military Cross and two bars; for this action he would receive, posthumously, the Victoria Cross.

His citation for a VC included the following:

'In Italy, on the night of 8th–9th April, 1945, Major Lassen was ordered to take out a patrol of one officer and seventeen other ranks to raid the north shore of Lake Comachio.

'His tasks were to cause as many casualties and as much confusion as possible, to give the impression of a major landing, and to capture prisoners. No previous reconnaissance was possible and the party found itself on a narrow road flanked on both sides by water.

'Preceded by two scouts Major Lassen led his men along the road towards the town. They were challenged after approximately five hundred yards from a position on the side of the road. An attempt to allay suspicion by answering that they were fishermen returning home failed, for when moving forward again to overpower the sentry, machine-gun fire started from the position, and also from the other blockhouses to the rear.

'Major Lassen himself then attacked with grenades, and annihilated the first position containing four Germans and two machine-guns. Ignoring the hail of bullets sweeping the road from three enemy positions, an additional one having come into action from three hundred yards down the road, he raced forward under covering fire from the remainder of the force. Throwing in more grenades he silenced this position which was then overrun by his patrol. Two enemies were killed, two captured, and two more machine-guns silenced.

'By this time the force had suffered casualties and its fire power was very considerably reduced. Still under a very heavy cone of fire Major Lassen rallied and reorganized his force and brought his fire to bear on the third position. Moving forward himself he flung in more grenades which produced a cry of "Kamerad". He then went forward to within three or four yards of the position to order the enemy outside and take their surrender.

'Whilst shouting to them to come out he was hit by a burst of Spandau fire from the left of the position and he fell mortally wounded but even whilst falling he flung a grenade, wounding some of the occupants and enabling his patrol to dash in and capture this final position.

'Major Lassen refused to be evacuated as he said it would impede the withdrawal and endanger further lives, and as ammunition was nearly exhausted the force had to withdraw.

'By his magnificent leadership and complete disregard for his own personal safety, Major Lassen had, in the face of overwhelming superiority, achieved his object. Three positions were wiped out, accounting for six machine-guns, killing eight and wounding others of the enemy, and two prisoners were taken. The high sense of devotion to duty, and the esteem in which he was held by the men he led, added to his own magnificent courage, enabled Major Lassen to carry out all the tasks he had been given with complete success.'

Lassen, of course, embodied all the qualities which made the SBS a success. He also embodied a few, such as a liking for stray and smelly dogs, and a casual disregard for military convention, which sometimes exasperated his fellow warriors. Ian Lapraik, who knew Lassen as well as anyone, thought that if he had not been killed and the war had not finished soon afterwards, Lassen would have been promoted and shown himself capable of exercising command at a high level. But undoubtedly he would have been profoundly bored by routine peace-time soldiering and staff work.

Lassen's finest qualities, which were not unique to him but shared by many of his SBS comrades, were speed of thought and movement, rapid reaction, and extreme coolness in the face of danger. A steady, brave, fast-thinking man has a much better chance of survival than a frightened or unsettled one does; that is obvious. However, it is not given to all human beings to be cool, brave and fast-thinking when in danger of losing their lives.

Lassen was not only an example to his men of leadership in battle, he was also deeply concerned for their welfare at all times. He never expected anyone to do more than (or as much as) he did himself. And if the need arose he would sacrifice his own life to save theirs. It did, and he did.

CHAPTER 10

The Other SBS

While following the fortunes of the SBS in the Mediterranean and to the north we have had to neglect the progress made by the other SBS in Britain. This had eventually been formally constituted by Major R. J. Courtney, MC, on 16th April 1942, with Captain G. C. S. Montanaro, R.E. as Second in Command and Chief Instructor. In 1940 Courtney had discussed with Admiral Sir Roger (later Lord) Keyes the possibilities of using canoes for reconnaissance and small raids in occupied Europe. He had been given permission to use the first Special Boat Section which had started training on the Isle of Arran with 8th Commando – their first operation had been against the coast of Holland in November 1940. In 1941 the unit, now known as Z Group, Special Boat Section, had two officers and four other ranks. It went to Alexandria where it began practising (as mentioned earlier in the book) and eventually became I SBS.

Montanaro was a regular officer in the Royal Engineers who had been at Cambridge (St Catharine's College) just before the war; he was an expert canoeist, and highly-qualified. Montanaro's 101 Troop (Army Commandos) were experts in canoeing, camouflage, infiltration and so on, skills which they had already displayed in a raid on Boulogne harbour in early 1942. Montanaro and his team were nothing if not ingenious. They had developed a way of attaching limpet mines to enemy ships by means of six-foot rods allowing the magnetic mine to be placed where the unsuspecting victim would not detect its presence till too late. Later he became a Lt Commander, Royal Navy, temporary. His career recalls that other most ingenious warrior, F. A. Brock, who was killed in the Zeebrugge raid of 1918. Brock was a Lt Colonel in the Army, Wing Commander in the RAF and Commander in the Royal Navy all at the same time.

Many of the 1942 SBS recruits came from Montanaro's Commando 101 Troop which had now been disbanded; their total strength amounted to forty-seven. Training was rigorous and included boom crossing and mine laying.

When Courtney's SBS was officially recognized it represented the culmination and co-ordination of many experiments. In the opening months of World War II when the general public was under the impression that hostilities would soon be concluded sensibly and fairly painlessly, there were fortunately a number of people who took a more realistic view. One of these was a certain H. G. 'Blondie' Hasler, a Major in the Royal Marines who had always had a passion for small boats. He was an individualist who liked to do long dangerous trips on his own, but he could co-operate well with others when the need arose. In early 1942 Hasler was with a small team at Southsea known as Combined Operations Development Centre: previously it had been called the Inter-Services Training and Development Centre. A year before he had put a paper to Combined Ops headquarters suggesting methods of attacking enemy craft by means of canoes and underwater swimming techniques. This, like many another bright idea, had been rejected as being too fanciful and shelved, but when in September 1941 a British naval tanker in harbour at Gibraltar was blown out of the water, to be followed by heavy damage to other ships outside the harbour, Hasler's papers were taken out, dusted and studied. In December of the same year similar explosions took place in Alexandria harbour. On this occasion two British battleships were put out of action by six Italians in two midget submarines. These alarming events were the culmination of a campaign which the Italians had been planning for a long time, and there was more to come.

Fortunately from the moment he came to power in 1940 Churchill had encouraged the idea of combined operations in which all the problems of attacking the enemy on a large or small scale should be worked out. He installed the then Captain Lord Louis Mountbatten as Chief of Combined Operations, although that particular appointment did not take place till March 1942. By the spring of 1942 it had been noted that there was a steady procession of boats from Japan carrying crude rubber to Germany and Italy; their port of entry was Bordeaux. Other valuable commodities were also using the same route, and this meant that the Axis needs in raw materials were being satisfactorily supplied. This would at least have protracted and might even have lost us the war.

Hasler was briefed to find a means of blowing up ships in the Gironde estuary and making it unnavigable; his subsequent adventures have been described in both book and film as *The Cockleshell Heroes*. Hasler objected strenuously to the title 'Cockleshell' but his views on the matter were ignored. The original folboats had been known as 'Cockle Mark I'. Mark Is were, as their name implies, collapsible; they could also be dismantled and packed into bags. Mark II, which Hasler favoured, had a rigid bottom but was light enough to be carried.

Although Hasler was pleased to find that Combined Operations had the blessing of the Chief of Staff, he felt that there were disadvantages in experimenting so publicly in the Solent. Their training was bound to attract attention. What was needed was some harmless but misleading term which could cover their activities and at the same time represent a compact little unit. He suggested that the most appropriate title would be Royal Marine Harbour Patrol Detachment. Mountbatten changed this title to Royal Marine Boom Patrol Detachment and this was officially established on July 6th 1942. Official establishment usually followed a long period of experimental work. This, as we saw earlier in the book, produced the frogmen who destroyed the German destroyers and other craft in Leros harbour when requested by the Mediterranean SBS to do so.

There were, of course, other units working with boats. There were the Royal Marine Commandos, Army Commandos, the Combined Operations Pilotage Parties and the Chariot and X Craft units.* Eventually another group, the Special Boat Unit, was formed for South East Asia Command, which included the RMBPD. The British-based SBS were always a Combined Operations unit, but in 1948 the SBS were transferred to the

---

* See Appendices II and VII.

Marines. Some of its personnel were ex-SAS; others were Marines.

By 1948 there had already been moves to put training in minor landing craft under the Royal Marines and this was now to be formally recognized, but there was a problem. During World War II the SBS had been developed in close cooperation with the SAS and there had been much interchange of personnel. There was clearly a need for continued cooperation, not rivalry, and a common doctrine was required. The SAS felt, not without reason, that if anyone was entitled to use the term Special Boat Squadron it was them, but they did not wish to be stuffy about it. It was decided that the Marines could use the title Special Boat Squadron as a purely functional title. However two years later the Small Raids Wing of the Amphibious School was reorganized and a small unit, known as the Special Boat Section, was formed under that title. The SAS thought this a confusing development but did not actively oppose it.

But to return to Courtney's SBS.

In 1943 it transferred to Titchfield Haven, near Fareham, Hampshire. Here they practised navigation both by day and night. By the end of 1943 training sites were at a premium in Britain, for everyone wanted to get into the best possible shape for the invasion of France that must soon take place. The SBS brief was to attack targets deep inland and survive on minimal rations. Strict and somewhat frustrating regulations had to be complied with. Targets such as other people's training camps had to be visited undetected and plastered with dummy charges. Part of the realism was lost because the targets would know they were to be attacked and would therefore take extra precautions; attacks on unwarned targets could well be met with live bullets, as everyone was well aware: if we could raid the Germans in France, the Germans might equally well wish to raid us in Britain. Although the fear of German parachute attacks which had been so noticeable in the dark days of 1940 had now diminished, it had not disappeared entirely. As regards survival, SBS troops were told they could live off the country to the extent of asking farmhouses for vegetables, but must not under any circumstances help themselves. A field of turnips and cabbages looks very tempting to a hungry man, who cannot imagine that a turnip would ever be missed but that turnip is, of course, somebody else's property. If offered rationed food, such as meat, tea, butter or eggs, soldiers were allowed to eat it, though they were not to ask for it. It is difficult some forty years later to realize that an egg a week was a luxury and 2 ounces of meat a standard ration. Nowadays, when survival techniques have been brought to a very high pitch of efficiency, a soldier will see many more eatable objects around him than turnips or cabbages in a farmer's field. As we said earlier, much of that derives from Philip Pinckney's experiments.

But the SBS, as it gained experience, came to be used for more hazardous and useful work. This was to examine the French beaches in different areas. The purpose of such reconnaissance was to find out the whereabouts, number and type of the French beach defences. This knowledge would be invaluable to the invasion forces which were to be landed in Normandy before Europe could be reconquered. The Germans were particularly ingenious with underwater obstacles; these varied from spikes and mines to wire and booby-trapped obstacles.

It was also necessary, in the dark and undetected, to take soundings of the depth of water off the coast. This was required for estimating how close in the bigger craft would be able to come. A major problem was that the Channel can be one of the roughest and most dangerous seas in the world; the beaches, as many a modern holidaymaker knows, can sometimes be changed dramatically during a storm and sand may replace shingle or vice versa.

The invasion force which was being planned, built and assembled needed certain types of information. The fleet which would eventually sail could be divided, roughly, into two different elements. The first was the larger ships such as the Landing Ships Tank, which could travel over rough water at a speed of some ten knots. Landing Ships Infantry, which were probably converted passenger or cargo ships, would be in the same category. Because of their size these could not go in too far or they would run aground with disastrous results. The point at which the larger vessels must stop was probably on charts but needed to be checked – an ideal job for the SBS. From that point Landing Craft Tank or Landing Craft Assault would take over. LCTs would unload tanks on the beach: LCAs would carry infantry as far in as possible. It was vital that the nearest point to the shore for this to happen should be established. Whereas if a large ship came in too close and ran aground it was a sitting target for enemy gunners and aircraft, so if an LCT or LCA was off-loaded too far out, the fact that it was heavy and flat-bottomed could cause it to be swamped or overturned in the rough seas. The seas on D Day were indeed rough.

The delicacy of this operation was shown by the misfortunes of the Americans off Omaha Beach. In order to make the transfer from larger ships to assault craft outside the range of the German shore batteries the Americans chose a point twelve miles out. The seas were much too rough for the flat-bottomed craft, and hundreds of men were drowned before they reached the beach.

All this vital information about currents and beaches had to be gathered and checked by men moving quietly at night off hostile coasts long before the invasion could take place. They, like their earlier comrades in the Mediterranean, would have to operate by being transported by submarines; one does not canoe across the Channel.

Another important area for research was the beaches themselves. When France fell there was a horrified realization that the British knew all too little of the French beaches. The information which was urgently required was the nature of the sand or shingle (or rock) and the degree of the slope. Having taken a tank some thirty miles across the Channel, and off-loaded it with a smaller craft, it would be a sad moment if the beach where it came ashore was so soft that it would sink into the sand or, alternatively, so steep that it would not be able to hoist itself along under its own power. Unbelievable though it may seem, the War Office had launched an appeal for picture postcards of French seaside resorts. The keen eyes of intelligence officers in the War Office would be less interested in the appearance of the pretty girl sitting in a deck chair than in the slope of the beach she was on, its apparent composition, and the nearness of the cliffs. But when all available information had been collected and analysed there was still a need for quiet men to engage in the prosaic but vital task of taking samples of sand and shingle off French beaches. War has many aspects.

The SBS in Britain wore battledress with a Commando/SBS flash. Their comrades in the Mediterranean wore the minimum of drab clothing and the SAS sand-coloured beret and badge, which dated from the days when the SBS had been under SAS command. Even though they were parted functionally, the two units never completely diverged, and after 1945 the SBS lived on in the SAS – for a time.

CHAPTER 11

Present Tense

After World War II, the second 'War to End War', a weary world breathed a sigh of relief and settled back to what it expected would be a long period of freedom from danger and worry. World War II had lasted six years and everyone was well sick of it. Looking backwards six years does not seem a long time; to imagine its effect one has to look forward. Imagine a war beginning in 1983 and dragging on till 1989. Rationing, black-out, deaths, destruction, separation, shortages of everything . . . No wonder there was a rush to get out of almost everything associated with World War II the moment the firing stopped.

Ships were scrapped or sold off to foreign governments still sufficiently misguided to think there could be a future for such things; men and women were demobilized; carefully constructed and ingenious plans for continuing the war were thrown away. No lessons were learnt from the previous war, when the Allies had disarmed recklessly while the Germans were laying the foundations for a brilliant armoured division and for military aircraft.

Unfortunately the general euphoria about peace did not seem to be matched by the Soviet Union. While the USA demobilized forces of eleven million, reducing them to 1½ million in a year and a half, the Soviet Union kept over four million men under arms and seemed more concerned than ever with extending her military strength. This was explained as being due to her fear of being invaded once more, but in view of the fact that her empire now sprawled across Europe, taking in Poland, Bulgaria, Romania and Hungary, this suggested that either the Soviets were over-sensitive or the West was particularly naïve.

Fortunately there were people in the Armed Forces of the West who felt that the expertise so carefully developed during the war should not be thrown or given away. They observed with interest that when sixteen Rolls Royce Nene engines were taken off the secret list by the Labour Government and sold to the Russians, the Russians studied them carefully and fitted them and others like them to their Migs which would be used so efficiently in the Korean War.

Although the SAS had not abandoned its interest in work with small boats and the like, in the 1950s the main centre of experiment in this field was with the Royal Marines. They carefully collected and collated the experimental data from the Second World War. There were good reasons to be wary of neglecting any bright ideas from the past. The ideas for midget submarines, frogmen and human torpedoes had all had their origin in British inventions developed earlier. Undoubtedly a lot of very foolish ideas are put up for consideration to the Ministry of Defence, but far too often in the past useful suggestions have been ignored or shelved. The tank is the classic example, and even when that was put into production there was so much prejudice against it from the more bone-headed senior officers that it was a long time before it was properly employed.

The Marines, like everyone else in the Armed Forces, were expected to make bricks with less and less straw as the hot war receded and the Cold War ground on its way. At the same time the character of war was changing.

Any future conflict was likely to be one of extremes. One extreme was huge air fleets, vast bombardments, massive carriers, tanks by the thousand, megaton explosions. These would undoubtedly be devastating but might they not all be fictions? The other extreme was a throwback to the very earliest days of human combat when a lone fighter, dependent on nothing but his own endurance and skill, could reach the centre of the enemy citadel. History abounds with such reso-lute people; the story of the Trojan horse is an early example. In 1203 Château Gaillard, the impregnable castle on the Seine, fell because an intrepid soldier crawled up through a drain and started a fire within the walls. In Cardiff, in the same century, a man who felt he had a grievance scaled the castle walls, evaded the garrison and the sentries, broke into the castle mound, kidnapped the owner, his wife and child, and conveyed them to a forest where he held them to ransom. Nowadays, perhaps, the more obvious targets are too well-guarded for the individual to emulate such feats (although President Sadat of Egypt clearly was not), but there are always others. The wheel seems to have turned full circle; we are back to the skills of the prehistoric hunter.

The new SBS had to forget nothing, but also to add a new set of ideas to tried experience. Its task has been described as to harass, to impede movement, to destroy stores, to report air targets, to blow up communications, to gain information, to do deep reconnaissance. Now it also has to know how to penetrate harbours and guarded places, swiftly, silently, unobserved.

For this certain skills are fundamental. The SBS man must be an expert navigator highly proficient at reading maps and aerial photographs. His signalling must be first-class. His powers of endurance must be considerable and he must have sufficient medical knowledge to look after himself and his comrades, even to the extent of minor surgery. He must be an expert in all methods of approaching the target, whether it be in the handling of small boats, underwater swimming, or by parachuting. Having arrived at his target he must be able to destroy it by the correct use of the right amount of explosive: too little or too much could be equally disastrous. There are of course more ways of crippling a target than blowing it to pieces, which is noisy and not always predictable.

He operates with equipment infinitely superior to anything known by his World War II predecessors. In the early days Montanaro and his men used to conceal themselves by standing up to their necks in Scottish rivers, and nearly froze to death in the process. Much of the early work of underwater swimming was done without any artificial aids. Nowadays when almost every child on a beach seems to have a pair of flippers and a snorkel, it is easy to forget how recent these inventions are. In the mid 1930s early experiments had clumsy foot attachments which opened as the foot was pushed back – or were meant to open. Wet suit, flippers, goggles, helmets, new forms of swimming stroke have now made the frogman's life much easier and that of his opponent more precarious.

Much the same applies on dry land. The raider's clothing is entirely different, being lighter, waterproof, more comfortable, more durable. He is able to produce hot meals from mini-cookers; his rations are light, sustaining, palatable. Everything he needs to use, whether it be a torch or water-purifying device, will be the best for the purpose.

The man himself will have been carefully selected and trained. About two-thirds fail the gruelling twelve-month training course. At the end of it he will be a good swimmer on or under water, capable of navigating any craft, a parachutist, an expert photographer, a demolition expert and a radio operator. If he's lucky he will have learnt to ski as well. Above all, he will know how to survive. Survival does not merely mean staying alive; it means staying alive and being able to perform whatever task is set, swiftly and efficiently. The early Italian frogmen used to reach their targets, lay their charges and give themselves up. The SBS man is required to fight another day, so when his work has been done he must be able to escape.

All this requires a special temperament. He may be a superman under stress but he must be a very ordinary person as well. A sense of humour is essential. He must be able to relax, to switch off. The man who will wake up in the night dreaming he has been trapped while cutting through underwater net is not the man for the SBS. In his mind work and play must be clearly separated.

Lastly, but first in importance, he must be intelligent. All sorts of super-toughs wish to join special forces, but the fact of life is that you can train intelligent people and make them tough but you are hard pressed to make a tough physical type intelligent unless his intelligence is underdeveloped rather than absent.

Fortunately there are plenty of volunteers with the right qualities. SBS men are not supermen. They are good all-rounders. Asked if their job is difficult, they will tell you 'There's nothing to it.' You can tell that to the Marines.

CHAPTER 12

Cold Water Work

Since 1950 the SBS have stayed out of the public eye as much as possible, an art now known as 'keeping a low profile' or 'playing your cards close to your chest'.

This is, of course, entirely understandable. Judging by Soviet activities in Afghanistan, the West is facing an enemy as ruthless as any in the history of the world. The Russians are not merely ruthless, they are relentlessly determined to develop their armed force in every sphere, from laser war in outer space to massed infantry attacks on the ground. They have not neglected underwater warfare, and have built and are continuing to build a formidable number of submarines large and small. For the last ten years Russian midget submarines have been testing their abilities in the coastal waters of neutral Sweden. The submarines employed near the Musko base in Sweden are known to be very small and equipped with caterpillar tracks which enable them to crawl on the bottom. These are clearly a development of the 'chariots', the two-man torpedo craft that were once directed to the targets by men riding them like horses at three knots an hour underwater; they are also related to the X craft mini-submarines of World War II. Thus it is clearly important not to reveal to the Russian navy more than they will have already learnt from traitors who have acted as Russian spies or from American technical magazines which make overfull use of the American Freedom of Information Act.

But in 1982 a corner of the veil over the SBS activities was lifted for a moment. The occasion was the Falklands War. The SBS had never been called on to work in quite such inhospitable conditions as that of the Falkland Islands, nor on such difficult territory.

The first problem about the Falklands War was distance: they were 8000 miles from Britain. Once the base on South Georgia had been lost there was no secure point from which operations could be launched. The second problem was the terrain. It was rocky, marshy, rugged, yet often bare – in fact as unsatisfactory as it could be. The third factor was the weather. This was the South Atlantic, not far from the Antarctic, cold, windy, wet, snowy, foggy. Altogether it represented, one might say, quite a challenge.

The background to the dispute has some relevance to subsequent events. The Falkland Islanders were British, but there were only 1800 of them. The islands were claimed by the Argentine on very dubious grounds but as Britain had been in continuous possession for over 150 years the British title was upheld by international law. On 2nd April 1982 the Argentine invaded the Falkland Islands with 2500 men and a fleet which included an aircraft carrier, three destroyers and several other ships. They came ashore without declaration of war at Port Stanley, where there was a force of eighty-four Royal Marines. The Marines, although surprised, fought back and killed fifteen of the invaders as well as wounding seventeen, without losses themselves; but being hopelessly outnumbered were ordered by the Governor to surrender in the face of impossible odds. On the following day another Argentine force invaded South Georgia 780 miles away where there were twenty-two Marines; these fought for seven hours and killed three Argentine soldiers. The Argentinians, who were governed by a ruthless though inefficient military dictatorship, assumed that once the islands had been occupied Britain would be glad to accept terms and a suitably Argentine-dominated future for the Falklands would be arranged.

Britain saw the matter differently, and immediately commissioned a Task Force of 100 ships and 28,000 men. Few people thought that Britain had the resolution, the ability or the means to launch the force or operate it under such difficult conditions. 'The Falklands' are a group of two hundred islands, 130 by 80 miles in extent. Half the area is land. The group lies 300 miles east of the tip of South America. A large area of South America is occupied by Argentina which is 2,300 miles long by

930 miles wide. It may seem extraordinary that such a vast country with such enormous resources should covet a barren group of islands some 300 miles off its coast, but that was what the Argentines did.

To the surprise of many, including the Argentines, the Task Force made its first landings on 21st April at Grytviken, South Georgia. Further landings took place on 20th and 21st May on East Falkland, one of the two largest islands.

But long before the Task Force had completed its 8000 mile journey the SBS and SAS were in action. As soon as the order was given, small groups landed on South Georgia and conducted a reconnaissance. The landings were not achieved without danger, which at times seemed close to disaster. The weather turned to blizzard and the isolated groups stood a very good chance of being frozen to death; however, they survived. Meanwhile other groups were busy on the East and West Falklands, noting the numbers of Argentines, the location of stores, the type of weapons employed. This information was particularly valuable, for the Argentinians were found to be much better armed than had been thought possible. Although some contact was made with the local people it was kept to the minimum.

When the Task Force landings took place the SBS were again actively engaged in creating diversions. At Grytviken they came ashore in frogmen's suits and set up a diversionary attack – this was necessary because the Task Force landing on the main Falkland Islands faced a considerable risk because they would be exposed to attack by the Argentine Air Force. The chosen spot was near Port San Carlos, in San Carlos Water, on the north-west coast of East Falkland. Here there had been an Argentine observation post, strongly garrisoned. The SBS disposed of it very quickly and efficiently, and the main landing was unopposed.

As they had been in action before the others arrived, it was essential that they should also be there for the last battle. The final objective was Port Stanley. Before the main attack went in a diversionary attack was mounted by SBS and SAS on Wireless Ridge, an important feature to the north-west of the port. It was not meant to hold the position but to draw the

Argentines out of their previous dispositions. It worked well. The Argentines attacked the SBS and SAS who withdrew, 2 Para then went in and captured the Ridge, and Port Stanley fell soon after.

The most traditional activity of the SBS was at Pebble Island, West Falklands where there was an important Argentine airfield. After landing by canoe the SBS joined up with the SAS, who had come in by helicopter, and the combined force moved on to the airfield. Eleven aircraft were destroyed in the time-honoured way of putting explosive charges on them. It was a far cry from the Greek islands but it worked as well as it had always worked.

In its existence of less than fifty years the SBS has established a tradition, a reputation and a history that may be equalled but is unsurpassed by any other unit in the world.

The Lesson of the Falklands was that in the SBS you must be prepared for anything, anywhere. The SBS was already aware of this fact, but the Falklands campaign certainly reinforced its thinking. The SBS, like other units, needs to think months, even years ahead, and of how to fight in the most unexpected places. Although in this book we have recorded many successes, there were of course operations which fell a long way short of success. Some in fact were complete disasters. For future planning the disasters afford better material for analysis than the successes.

Among the less successful ventures were the attempts to recce the Scheldt estuary in 1944; here the weather proved a major obstacle. Although the SBS were never properly engaged in the Far East, others, such as the COPPS and SRUs (Sea Reconnaissance Units) were. The Far East operations showed up a whole fresh set of problems. Many of them, such as the hostile creatures in the water, the climate and the alertness of the Japanese, were encountered by Detachment 385, a group from RMBPD who arrived late in the war in February 1945. These canoeists were also parachutists, but in the event were landed from a Catalina flying boat and HDMLs. Some were killed in action, some drowned, some captured, some summarily shot after capture.

Wartime experience was put to use and supplemented during the Malayan 'Emergency' of 1948–60. The 'Emergency' had begun in 1945 when planters and tappers were murdered, trees slashed, and tin mines sabotaged. At first this was thought to be the work of a few dozen communist terrorists. Experience soon showed that the opposition was on a much larger scale: eventually over six thousand terrorists were killed and three thousand captured. Malaya is four-fifths jungle but produces approximately one-third of the world's supply of natural rubber and over fifty per cent of the world's tin. The terrorists lived in camps deep in the jungle and obtained food from Malay villages. After a successful excursion for murder and destruction they would retire to their jungle hide-outs.

Hunting them, the SBS found themselves less frequently in canoes on rivers than on their feet in jungle and scrub. But the SBS man is nothing if not an all-rounder: war, like peace, is indivisible. In Malaya the SBS acquired much knowledge and experience of counter-terrorist work, of approaching difficult targets, and of working in a climate where their worst enemies often seemed to be the smallest – the mosquitos and the leeches.

As the Malayan Emergency was building up, a fresh challenge appeared in the shape of the Korean War. This had begun when North Korea invaded South Korea on 25th June 1950; the United Nations promptly voted for its members to assist South Korea in expelling the invaders. The brunt of the task was accepted by the United States but a force was sent from the Commonwealth, and a small group of SBS assisted in a deception landing made some distance from the Inchon landing of September 1950. This small group, under the command of the then Lieutenant, but later Major-General E. G. D. Pounds of the Royal Marines, stayed with the US forces in the area after the successful Inchon landing. This group, incidentally, was not a regular SBS unit but one formed for the purpose from volunteers already in the theatre.

In the 1960s developments in Indonesia produced a situation in which the SBS could take a more conventional rôle. Indonesia is a group of 10,000 islands, of which Sumatra, Java and Borneo are the largest. In 1963 President Sukarno of

Indonesia decided to 'liberate' certain territories from the newly-created rival state of Malaysia. They included former British North Borneo and Sarawak. As Britain had a defence treaty with the Federation of Malaysia, British forces immediately went to the aid of the threatened territories. The Sabah (former British North Borneo) border with Indonesia was a network of rivers, jungle, mangrove swamp and steep ridges. It was ideal country for border raiding – if you knew where the border was, and few people did. Indonesian soldiers made full use of the opportunities for infiltration, and British forces occupied themselves intercepting them or cutting off their retreat. In this 'confrontation', as it was called, the SBS canoeists took a useful part in reconnaissance and ambushing.

For political and military reasons the details of the Indonesian campaign are still regarded as 'sensitive' and are thus not available for publication. Subjects which are politically sensitive are often those in which opinions expressed in secret documents at the time might be prejudicial to future good relations with past adversaries. Matters which are militarily sensitive relate to policy, methods, tactics, or weapons employed. The assumption that after thirty years all details will be revealed, as all relevant papers will have been put in the Public Records Office, is unfortunately not quite true. Relevant files are often 'weeded', which means that 'papers whose disclosures would not be in the public interest' are destroyed. Weeding is regarded with deep suspicion by historians, who suspect that it is often used to remove evidence of blunders and miscalculations, the revealing of which would be damaging to certain careers.

The aim of this book has been to give a fair account of the successes and failures of a body of men of exceptional talents and dedication. It does not speculate on the future. Small boat and underwater warfare will obviously be even more demanding for highly-qualified performers than it has in the past. They will, of course, have the benefit of the latest scientific and technical aids; against them undoubtedly will be defence no less up-to-date. But, as we said in the first chapter, the wheel has turned full circle and although wars are now conducted with every form of possible scientific, electronic, and even psychological devices, they still need the skill of the primitive hunter. The primitive hunter had to find and stalk his prey, and not become prey himself. Having reached his objective he needed to have sufficient strength, skill and cunning to outwit and kill his enemy.

In all probability he could see over long distances as well as modern man can with binoculars (some primitive people still can), see at night as well as an SBS man can with an image intensifier, and sense the presence of danger as clearly as if he had an electronic scanner. His ability at swimming and diving was perhaps matched to the fish he had to catch.

The reward was survival. It remains so to-day.

APPENDIX I
The Cockleshells

The full story of the feat of Lt Colonel H. G. Hasler and his fellow Marines is told in a book entitled *The Cockleshell Heroes*, written by C. E. Lucas-Phillips, OBE, MC, published by Heinemann in 1956. A film had already been made of the exploit by Warwick Films (Columbia Pictures) in which Trevor Howard and Josè Ferrer played the leading parts; the whole cast was put through a full course of training by the Royal Marines, and some reached full Marine standards. The film was made on the River Tagus rather than the Gironde for technical reasons.

The 'Cockleshell' operation took place in December 1942. Five canoes were embarked on the submarine *Tuna* on 30th November, and *Tuna* proceeded down the Irish Sea and along the Bristol Channel on the surface. A Force 4 wind made the submarine roll, and the passengers were sick. When she reached enemy-patrolled water, she submerged by day and came up at night. Disembarking on the night of the 7th was a delicate operation, as there were enemy aircraft and patrol boats in the area.

The canoes were 16 feet long with a beam of 28½ inches and a depth of 11¼ inches. They could collapse to a depth of 6 inches. Each weighed 90 lbs. Each had a flat bottom of 1/8th inch plywood. A canoe could be dragged fully-loaded over a beach without harm if necessary, or could be launched from the beach itself so that it went into the water with its two-man crew on board. The deck was plywood and was held up by eight struts, three to a side and one each at bow and stern.

The sides were rubberized fabric. The men sat in a central cockpit covered with waterproof fabric on seats one inch from the floor. They carried a bailer and a sponge, a magnetic compass, painters (ropes) at bow and stern, and two pairs of double paddles; the paddle could be pulled apart to make two single paddles if necessary. The central joint was adjusted so that each blade was at right angles to the other, which meant that when one blade was in the water the other blade was 'feathered' by having its edge to the wind. The man in the forward seat was in command and was responsible for steering. Using double paddles meant much faster progress but made the canoe more noticeable; the dripping water also made a certain amount of noise. Single paddling was slower but quieter, and avoided the silhouette effect.

Buoyancy was given by 'buoyancy bags' in the bow and stern. These were a mixed blessing. They kept the canoe afloat although it could be flooded and capsize in rough water. (It could not be rolled over like a kayak for that would mean abandoning the stores). Furthermore, the buoyancy made it almost impossible to sink when the canoeists wished to abandon the canoe and swim ashore. In the Mediterranean buoyancy bags were made up of table tennis balls.

Paddling canoes in rough seas over long distances was extremely arduous. In a boat or canoe (and, I believe, on a tandem bicycle!) when conditions are bad, it is difficult to believe that a partner or partners are making any effort at all: unwarranted suspicion develops into raging conviction. Navigation in rough sea on dark nights was also a major problem. Sometimes, whether the navigator was expert or not, canoeists could find themselves stuck in soft mud. There was a complicated and arduous technique for sliding over this, but soft mud was a constant hazard.

There were of course other problems, not unlike those faced by present-day astronauts. What food can be taken for maximum value? How much water? And what about natural functions? Urinating was possible with the bailing bowl, but anything else had to wait till you reached land.

Of the five canoes which set out two were captured soon after they left the submarine (which had been spotted by German radar). The ten mile journey to the mouth of the estuary and the sixty miles up the Gironde led to the loss of two more canoes. Four men, including Hasler, reached the target area and blew up a number of ships, then the remaining pair separated to make their way back through France and Spain. Only Hasler and his companion, Marine Sparks, escaped. Six of the others were shot by the Gestapo in cold blood; two seem to have been drowned for they were never heard of again.

The raid was a fantastic achievement – in its concept, in its execution, and in the bravery shown by all who took part. Those who were so infamously murdered by the Gestapo refused to give away any details of how the raid had been carried out.

APPENDIX II
Frogmen and Midget Submarines

In July 1941 the Italians attempted to attack shipping in Malta harbour, using two 'two-men torpedoes'; one of the 'torpedoes' was destroyed and the crew of the other was captured. The Italians had been experimenting with human torpedoes since 1935. Their torpedoes were 22 feet long, 21 inch wide cigar-shaped craft, which had detachable warheads carrying 500 lbs of explosive. They were driven by batteries and had two men sitting astride: they could not travel at more than 3 knots or the men would be swept off.

The torpedo usually travelled to its target with the men sitting with their chins just above the water, but they submerged and travelled by compass when close in. They descended under the target ship and detached the warhead, which was then attached to the ship. The crew then set course away from the ship: the explosion would take place between two and two and a half hours later.

The Royal Navy was now well aware that there were likely to be a continuation of such attacks – as indeed there were; volunteers were requested for diving duties in 1942.

A small team was created by Lt William Bailey, and Lt L. K. P. 'Buster' Crabb. This had a variety of duties, which included clearing propellers and recovering dead bodies – it recovered the bodies and vital papers when General Sikorsky's aircraft crashed into the sea at Gibraltar. It soon became clear to the Navy that underwater warfare had many aspects. By this time the Italians had divers who posed as seamen from neutral ships in neutral ports, but once night fell the innocent seamen became less innocent frogmen and swam out to Allied ships to which they attached limpet bombs by means of clamps or magnets. Obviously, if the ship then blew up in port, suspicion would be aroused, so either the bombs were set with very long time fuses or worked by small expendable propellers (a vane mechanism) which would last till the victim ship was well out to sea.

The Italians had many successes before their plans were countered. They displayed amazing ingenuity; on one occasion they cut a hole in the hull of one of their ships which had been scuttled in Algeciras harbour and used this as an exit for frogmen and torpedoes to move out and attack ships in Gibraltar. After the Italian armistice several of the Italian frogmen voluntarily joined the British team which was now commanded by 'Buster' Crabb. Some of these were happily employed in looking for unexploded mines at the bottom of harbours. Crabb, who was not only a good organizer and leader but also a very good diver, had been failed for the Navy on medical grounds when he had volunteered in 1939. He promptly joined the Merchant Navy as a carpenter, a post for which there was no medical exam. From the Merchant Navy he managed to transfer to the Royal Navy, again bypassing the doctor.

When Britain took up underwater warfare the operational area was at first the temperate waters of the Mediterranean but later the less hospitable or hostile waters of the North Sea, particularly around Norway. New underwater suits had to be designed. Not least of the problems was that of breathing: it is possible to die from oxygen poisoning as easily as from carbon dioxide poisoning.

An urgent requirement was an attack on the German battleship *Tirpitz*, anchored in a Norwegian fjord. The first vehicle had been two-man submarines, after the Italian model, known as 'Chariots'. These were now followed by X craft (first launched on 15th March 1943), which were midget submarines with a crew of four. They were larger than the human torpedoes, being 48 feet long and 5 ft 6 in diameter. The crew accommodation was 35 ft by 5 ft. Fully loaded they weighed 39 tons. They were driven by Diesel engines on the surface, giving a speed of 6½ knots. When submerged they were propelled by a battery-driven motor and could attain a speed of 4½ knots. They were, in fact, miniature submarines in everything but torpedo tubes: instead they carried two explosive charges alongside (side cargoes). Each charge contained two tons of amatol. They could stay under water for thirty-six hours at considerable depths, and could withstand the worst possible weather. They would creep into harbours, let out frogmen from the escape hatch, re-embark them when their charges had been laid, and return. Sometimes a diver would emerge from the X craft moored alongside a harbour net (some thirty feet below the surface), cut through the net with cutters powered from inside the X craft, and then guide the submarine as it passed through the hole he had cut. Then he would re-enter it via the escape hatch. Once inside a net, if detected, the chances of emerging were slight – but some managed to do so.

By the time of D Day, 6th June 1944, the frogmen in company with many others had already been at work surveying and clearing the routes into Normandy. One of the major achievements was that of the two midget submarines which acted as marker buoys from forty-eight hours before the invasion. They flashed coloured lights to the incoming invasion fleet, thus guiding in the leading groups. Eventually they had spent seventy-six hours at sea, sixty-four of them under water.

Frogmen and midget submarines were involved in several other operations before the war ended, not only in Europe but also in the Far East against Japanese ships. Although midget submarines were outside the province of the SBS, many of the other underwater activities of the Navy are of considerable interest to it. Likewise, all three services like to keep an eye on what the others are doing. There is, of course, inter-service rivalry, but this is beneficial in the long run because it stimulates each service to try fresh ideas and engage in flexible planning. It is a challenge for a man in one arm of the services to be able to take on a job from another service – whether it be flying, sailing, underwater swimming, parachuting, navigating – and to do it as well if not better than the man who does it as part of his job.

APPENDIX III
Weapons

The SBS used Brens, American 300 Carbines, and .303 Lee-Enfield Sniper's Rifles with telescopic sights. There was a proportion of one sniper's rifle to ten men; they were mainly used in ambushes. The Bren had a range of 2000 yards but was usually fired at targets at about 600 yards. It was reliable but tended to overheat unless the barrel was changed after using ten magazines. Brens were originally .303 but were later changed to 7.62; their firing speed was 500 rounds per minute. The Lee-Enfield .303 was the standard issue rifle for World War II (and World War I) and, even unmodified was accurate and effective at 1,000 yards – it has been used at ranges up to one mile. Its disadvantage was that it was reloaded by a bolt action, and moving the bolt to put in a fresh round could draw attention to the firer. Its maximum firing rate, not often achieved, was fifteen rounds per minute. It was not a difficult weapon to use and was extremely accurate, but its length and weight made it too cumbersome for mobile troops.

The 'Tommy gun' (Thompson sub-machine-gun) was a heavy, fast-firing (725 r.p.m.) gun which used .45 rounds. It had a range of up to 300 yards but was only accurate over much shorter distances. Its heavy-calibre round gave it what came to be called 'great stopping power'. The 300 Carbine, on the other hand, though lighter and easier to handle, would not stop an advancing enemy unless a bullet hit him in a vital organ. Stens were lighter, 9 mm, 500 r.p.m.; they had a range of 175 yards but were unstable.

Of the smaller guns Colt .45s were very popular, again with 'great stopping power'.

Unofficially the Luger (9 mm, automatic, short-range) and the Walther P.38 and Schmeisser Machine-Pistol (9 mm, 32 round magazines, 500 r.p.m. and a range of 150 yards) were popular and well-used. Captured Italian Breda machine-guns were also used. The advantage of using the enemy's weapons is that if you advance you are likely to obtain more ammunition easily, whereas ammunition for your own make of gun may not be following closely enough behind you.

Grenades of every type were popular, but the most widely used was the 36 (the Mills bomb) which weighed 1½ lbs and was thrown or lobbed into all sorts of places where it was likely to be unwelcome: dugouts, tank turrets, gun emplacements, ships, bunkers. It had a four-second fuse and was normally considered devastating at a radius of twenty-five yards; on a hard surface it could be lethal at much greater distances. The nightmare about grenades was that they could bounce or roll back towards the thrower.

Mortars had first come into use for firing into enemy trenches; subsequently they were found indispensable for hitting targets behind any form of barrier. Mortars could be extremely accurate when handled by experienced men.

2": Range 500 yards, 2½ lbs H.E., or 2 lbs smoke

3": Range 2,800 yards, 10 lbs H.E. or equivalent

4.2" Range 4,100 yards, but heavy to handle (weighed 257 lbs)

81 mm: Range 3,000 yards.

Mortars could not fire at a target *less* than 100 yards distant.

APPENDIX IV
The Stuka Dive Bomber

The Junkers Ju 87 B2 'Stuka' was widely used by the Germans in the early years of World War II and was particularly effective against shipping. It had a wing span of 45 feet, a length of 36.1 feet, and a 1400 h.p. Junkers Jumo 211 D engine. It carried 1540 lbs of bombs and was also armed with three 7.9 machine-guns. It had a crew of two and its cruising speed was 232 m.p.h. Its particular ability was to dive at a target while machine-gunning, and to release a bomb at the last moment from a very low altitude.

APPENDIX V
Colonel J. N. Lapraik, DSO, OBE, MC

Colonel John Lapraik, nicknamed 'Ian', who eventually received the surrender of the Germans in the Aegean, had a career which no one who had seen him as a boy, crippled by illness, could have imagined. Although he took up running with considerable success he was considered too 'fragile' to play the more vigorous games at Glasgow University, nor was he thought fit enough to be able to join the OTC. However, when war came he joined the army on the day of the outbreak (3rd September 1939) and began his military life in the ranks of the Highland Light Infantry. He was then sent to the Officer Cadet Training Unit at Dunbar (one of the more formidable OCTUs) and commissioned in the Cameron Highlanders. He was posted to the Middle East where he joined Middle East Commando. M. E. Commando had two battalions, 51 and 52, and Lapraik was in 51. This was mainly made up of Jews and Arabs, plus some Spaniards who had fought in the Civil War and had subsequently left Spain. M. E. Commando was a hard unit which fought with great success in the Abyssinian campaign but was then disbanded for political reasons. Lapraik recalls that Jews and Arabs worked in perfect harmony. Jews never fought in private fights against Arabs, though Jews sometimes fought against Jews, Arabs against Arabs, and the Spaniards among themselves or against anyone else.

After the disbanding of the Commando, Lapraik was posted to Malta to train the Malta garrison in Commando tactics, and originated raids on the German- and Italian-held section of the North African coast. This involved much canoeing for beach reconnaissance. Although he had little experience of boats before the war he developed a special liking for canoes. When he began canoeing his chest was 37 inches; when he finished it was 43. He once took a canoe from Malta to Sicily, a distance of some seventy miles, and on another occasion managed a canoe successfully in a Force 9 gale. He considered that 'anything above Force 6 made canoeing difficult'. While in Malta, Lapraik was near the submarine base, so he organized a unit which could operate from submarines.

Although only a selection of raids are described in the text, raiding parties were in action continuously and on most of the main islands the SBS had a patrol with a wireless set constantly at work. This meant that virtually every move the Germans or Italians made in the Aegean was observed and reported. Latterly the squadron worked in sections of twelve men.

On one occasion when they were sheltering in Turkish waters, Lapraik was arrested by the Turkish authorities and spent three weeks in a Turkish goal. The cause was a certain Turk who had been spying on the SBS activities and reporting on their strength to the Germans in Rhodes. As no body could be found Lapraik was released after three weeks, but the spying had stopped.

Before the invasion of Sicily the SBS was ordered to land on the island and take a prisoner. Lapraik led a patrol inland to a gun-site where an Italian soldier was singing merrily. He was grabbed by the SBS but not knocked unconscious, as they wanted him to walk the three miles back to the canoes. Back on the beach, they had a problem in finding somewhere on a canoe to stow the frightened prisoner. The solution was found by jettisoning the extra buoyancy bags (the table tennis balls) and fitting the Italian into the space thus freed. Fortunately he was not a large man.

Lapraik's narrowest escape came near Stampalia when their launch was lying up, camouflaged, close to the shore. Suddenly a German destroyer appeared round the headland. The MTB skipper gave two orders: 'Open fire' and 'Abandon ship'. On 'Open fire' they cleared the bridge of the destroyer; on 'Abandon ship' disappeared into the scrub on the island.

After the war Lapraik went on to command 21 SAS (Artists). On 8th October 1945 the SAS had been officially disbanded, but was re-formed in 1947 under the command of Lt Col B. M. F. Franks, DSO, MC, TD, who had previously commanded 2 SAS. It linked up with the Artists Rifles. Lapraik was the pioneer of overseas training, which later became a feature of all Army training. One of the reasons for his success was his belief that 'You should never underwork a unit'.

APPENDIX VI
Major T. B. Langton, MC, DL

When Langton was in Tobruk (after the first relief), he and the other members of the SBS experimented with embarkation into canoes from Motor Torpedo Boats. This was much more difficult than embarking from submarines, as the MTBs were much higher out of the water. One night they were sent for because a German aircraft had crashed on an island just off Gazala point. It was said to have a lot of secret material on board, so Langton set off on an expedition with two canoes to salvage what they could. The other canoe contained a newly-joined officer from the Scots Guards named Grant-Wilson, and James Sherwood. They were taken out by MTB and managed to launch their canoes, but it was a very rough night and Langton's canoe began to break up in the surf. He shouted to the other canoe and was answered by Grant-Wilson, who said they were all right and would go on. Langton managed to return to the MTB and obtained an inflatable dinghy which he paddled ashore.

On shore, they started looking for the other two. Suddenly they noticed there was a line of troops coming up behind them. They assumed they had lost the race to reach the missing plane. The oncoming troops surrounded them and were speaking in a foreign langauge among themselves. They called out to Langton to surrender, using a well-known British Army word in the context. Obviously they were not Germans – but who were they? They were soon enlightened – they were South Africans who had been speaking in Afrikaans.

However, as they appreciated their good fortune in being with their own side they also realized that the MTB had landed them on the mainland, not the island. It was, of course, a very rough dark night. They then heard a shout out at sea. Langton promptly re-embarked in his dinghy and paddled out to find Sherwood (then a Sergeant, later commissioned) on the other side of a reef where their canoe had capsized.

In the water, Grant-Wilson, who was not a particularly good swimmer, had taken off his life-jacket and insisted on giving it to Sherwood. Grant-Wilson soon disappeared below the water but Sherwood held on to him. When Langton reached Sherwood the latter was apparently too exhausted to help himself, and this made the task of rescue very long and difficult. When Langton finally got Sherwood to safety he was astonished to find that he was still clinging to the body of Grant-Wilson, who had been dead for some time.

When asked how he came to decide to try to walk from Tobruk to Cairo, Langton's reply was: 'Well, there was nothing else I could do. The thing I wanted less than anything was to be taken prisoner.' In order to get away from Tobruk more easily, his party split up into small groups. He started off with seven. Between them they had two pieces of chocolate, four biscuits, a little cheese, and four pints of water. They drank any water they could find in the radiators of wrecked trucks or tanks. Initially they were heading for a point on the coast north of Bardia where they had been told, if the worst came to the worst, that they could be picked up from the sea. However, when they arrived the Germans were already there. They moved back and found a friendly Arab village where they stayed for a while. Steiner – who assumed the name of Hillman – spoke fluent Arabic. Of the seven, one got lost and three who were too sick to continue walked on a road used by the Germans in order to be picked up and made prisoner but their numbers were reinforced by Pte Watler who had reached an Arab village and was waiting there. Langton had a small compass and navigated mostly by the stars. Unknowingly they crossed the German lines behind the November battle of Alamein. When they moved south, Langton felt that if they could skirt along the side of the Qattara Depression, a dried-up sea with a thin cake of salt on the surface, they could avoid the Germans and Italians, and work their way round to the road to Cairo.

143

They slid down a slope into the depression, which is due south of Alamein, and went to sleep. When they woke up they were surrounded by wild camels. When Langton's party began to move, the camels moved off across the salt crust. Realizing that this was one of the few firm tracks, Langton's party followed and came out near Himeimat. Here they met a party of Royal Engineers, clearing mines. At first Langton's party had tried to avoid them, thinking they might be German.

Langton lost five stone during the walk, but soon recovered. It was generally agreed that his determination and leadership had kept the party going and alive. The worst part, he thinks in recollection, was the cold at night when they shivered in their lice-ridden clothes.

APPENDIX VII
COPPS

COPPS were Combined Operations Pilotage Parties. They originated in September 1942 to reconnoitre the coast of what was then French North Africa in preparation for the 'Torch' landings (8th November 1942). They were recruited from Royal Engineers, who would be qualified to report on the beach constituents, and naval personnel who would be experienced in navigation. Unfortunately in the early stages their abilities as canoeists were limited, and a number were drowned; their task was partly taken over by SBS.

Later, in late 1943 and early 1944, COPPS took part in the surveys of the Normandy beaches and also performed the same function for the 'Anvil' landings in southern France (15th August 1944). COPPS operated in small groups in various other areas, including the Arakan and Akyab (Burma), the Malayan west coast, Sumatra, and the beach at Anzio. They also surveyed beaches in Sicily, at Salerno and in north-west Europe. They were not SBS, but they performed a comparable task.

Index

A

Adriatic, 6, 9, 87
Afghanistan, 123
Alamein, 35, 37
Albania, 9, 87
Allot, Cpt. K., 21–2, 26, 30
Amorgos, 82
Andartes, as blockade breakers,
    100
Anderson, Cpt., 69, 70, 71
Appleyard, Cpt. Geoffrey, 39
Araxos, 93
Argentina, and Falklands, 123–6
Army Commandos, 114
Athens, SBS in, 101
Auchinleck, Field Marshal, Sir
    Claude, 24, 35

B

Badoglio, Marshal, 43
Bailey, Lt. William, 133
Balbo, Marshal, 23
Balsillie, Lt. K., 60, 75, 97
Barnes, George, 29, 69
Barr, Cpt., 20
Belgium, 8
'Benghazi Handicap', 24
Berge, Commandant, 26–7
Bishop, Prvt., 57
Blyth, Cpt., 77
Boat-building, British tradition, 7
Booth, Cpl., 14, 20–1, 29
Boy's Own Paper, 7

Brinkworth, Cpt., 61, 62
Britain, 8, 10–11, 23, 24
Brock, Lt. Col. F. A., 112–3
Buck, Cpt., 36
'Bucketforce', 93
Bury, Lt. Bob, 64–5, 99

C

Calchi, 77
Campioni, Admiral, 48–50, 51
Cape Ras-el-Tin, 21
Cator, Col. H. J., 38
Chamberlain, Neville, 11
Channel Islands, 8–9, 11
Chariot Unit, 114
Chetniks, 89, 90
Churchill, Winston, 11, 13, 24,
    42–3, 52, 80, 113
Clark, Lt. David, 69, 70
Clarke, Lt. Col. Dudley, 11
Clarke, Lt. Gordon, 74, 80, 82,
    83
Clausewitz, 106
Cockleshell Heroes, 114, 130–2
Combined Operations Pilotage
    Parties, 114
Commando Training, 11–12
Commando 101 Troop, 112–3
COPPS, 126, 145
Corsica, 61
Cos, 71, 100
Costi, Lt., 26, 29
Courtney, R. J., 12, 13, 14, 19,
    112

Crabb, Lt. L. K. P. 'Buster', 133
Crete, 14, 18, 26–9, 45, 67
    attack on, 100–101
Cyclades, 80, 83

D

Dante's Inferno, 108
Denmark, 8
Dodecanese, 10, 51–61, 70, 83
Doenitz, Admiral, 52
Dolbey, Mjr., 48–9
Duncan, Cpt., 20, 29

E

Eastern Approaches, 39
EDES, 95–9
Egypt, 23
Eighth Army, 106
ELAS, 95–101, 200, 202
Ethiopia, 23
Evans, Pvt., 77

F

Falkland Islands, 123–6
Fanetza, Col., 50–1
Feebery, Cpl., 17, 26
Flavell, Sgt., 90
'Folboat Section', 12, 13, 15
France, 8
Freedom of Information Act, 123

G

Geary, Sgt., 64
German reprisals, against
    Greeks, 81–2
    tactics, against SBS, 75, 76
Gibraltar, 113
Grant, Donald, 75
Grant-Wilson, Guardsman, 142–4

Greaves, Cpl., 46–7, 57
Greece, 9, 18, 42, 67–8
    evacuation of, 12
    SBS in, 93–111
Greek Islands, strategic
    importance of, 42–3, 44–5
Greek Sacred Squadron, 30, 33,
    82, 85, 86
Grytviken, 125

H

Harden, Lt., 72, 73
Haseldene, Lt. Col., 35
Hasler, Major H. G. 'Blondie',
    113
Henshaw, Lt., 103
Hitler, Adolf, 8, 9, 23, 42, 53
Holland, 8
Holmes, Sgt., 103
Hughes, Marine, 11, 12, 14–15,
    19–20

I

Indonesia, 127–8
Ios, 81, 82
ISBS, 112
Istria, 104–6
Italian surrender at Skala, 75

J

Japan, 25
Jellicoe, Captain The Earl, 25,
    26–7, 29, 32, 38, 39, 48–9,
    50, 93, 94, 96, 101
Jones, Pvt., 77

K

Kalymnos, 76, 85
Kasako, Mjr. P., 85

Kealey, Cpt. M., 19, 26
Kesterton, Sgt., 48–9
Keyes, Admiral Sir Roger, 11, 112
Keyes, Lt. Geoffrey, 15–16
King, Admiral, 43
Korean War, 127

L

Landing Craft Assault, 117
Landing Craft Tank, 117
Landing Ships Infantry, 116
Landing Ships Tank, 116
Langton, Lt. T. B., 17, 32–3, 34, 35, 39, 142–4
Lapraik, Cpt. J. N., 45, 51–2, 54, 56, 57, 65, 84, 85, 100, 139–41
Lassen, Anders, 39, 40, 45, 46, 47, 51, 52, 54, 56, 68, 77, 80, 83, 88, 99–100, 101, 106, 107, 108, 109, 110
Laycock, Col. Robert, 12
'Layforce', 12, 15
Lecomber, Rifleman, 103
Leros, 70, 86
Lewes, Jock, 27, 28, 61
Libya, 9, 20, 23
Lodwick, Lt. John, 19, 74, 75, 81
Long Range Desert Group, 6, 105
Love and War in the Apennines, 19
Lussin, raid on, 102
Luxembourg, 8

M

Macbeth, Cpt. S., 84
Maclean, Fitzroy, 39, 45, 89
Malaya, 127
Malta, 133
Maund, Admiral, 13
Mayne, Lt. Col. R. B., 38

McGonigal, Lt. A., 90, 102, 104, 105
Medway, 12, 37
Mihailovich and Chetniks, 89
Miller, Sgt., 77
Milner-Barry, Walter, 55
Mitford, Cpt. Bruce, 70
Montanaro, Cpt. G. C. S., 19, 112
Monte St Angelo, 88
Montgomery, Field Marshal, 24, 35
Mountbatten, Cpt. Lord Louis, 113–4
Mussolini, Benito, 9, 23, 42, 43, 83
Myers, Gen. E. C. W., 95
Mykonos, 87

N

National Liberation Front (EAM), 95
Navarino, 19–20
Naxos, 83
Newby, Eric, 19, 29
Nicholas, Sgt., 46–7
Nisyros, 71–4, 76
Norway, 8, 42

O

O'Connor, Gen. Sir Richard, 23, 34
Omaha Beach, 117
O'Reilly, Guardsman, 107
Ogulin, 104

P

Pantallaria, 12
Papandreou, George, 96
Papanikolis, 30
Parry-Jones, Lt., 102

Patmos, 70, 74–5
Patras, raid on, 94
Patterson, Ian, 66, 67, 71, 72, 73, 93, 94, 97, 98, 101
Pelopennese, Allied strategy in, 93
Pebble Island, 126
Pelagos, 84
Phantom, 18
Phillips, Cpt. Gustavus March, 39
Pinckney, Philip, 40–1, 116
Piscopi, 71
Poland, 8, 119
Port San Carlos, 125
Port Stanley, 124
Pounds, Lt. E. G. D., 127

R

Ramsaur, Lt-Cmndr., 72–3
Rhodes, 12
  raid on, 30, 47–8
Rice, Pvt., 77
Riddiford, Cpt. D., 105
Riel, Louis, 2
Ritchie, Lt. D., 21–2
Rommel, Field Marshal Erwin, 9, 23–4, 34–5, 37
  plan to assassinate, 15–17
Roosevelt, Franklin, D., 80
Royal Marine Boom Patrol Detachment, 86, 114
Royal Marine Commando, 114
Rowe, Lt., 45

S

Sadat, President Anwar, 121
Salonika, 99–200
Santorini, 80
  raids on, 81
Sardinia, 61

SAS (Special Air Service), 6–7, 18–19
  attack on Cyrenica, 26
  relationship with SBS, 38
SBS (Special Boat Service) in the Adriatic, 88–92
  in Britain, 112–8
  official recognition of, 19
  philosophy, 37
  postwar, 119–129
  raids, effects of, 79
  and SAS, 25, 29
  scope of activities, 80
  training, 115–16, 122
  and Tobruk raid, 32–4
  and weapons, 136–7
Scopolod, 99
Scotland, 11
Scutari, 14
Seafaring, British tradition, 5
Sherwood, Lt. James, 14, 29, 142, 143
Sicily, 14, 42, 61, 63, 71
Sikorsky, Gen., 133
Simi, 64–6, 69, 85, 86, 100
Smith, Lt., 90
Smugglers, 4–5
SOE, 18, 64, 89
Somaliland, 23
South Georgia, 124, 125
Sparks, Marine, 132
Special Interrogation Group (SIG), 36
Spies, 18
Sporades, 10
SRU, 126
S-Squadron, 80
Stampalia, 69, 74–5
Steiner, Col., 36
Stellin, Lt., 52, 87, 108
Stephenson, Sgt., 73, 74
Stirling, David, 5–6, 18, 20, 26, 27, 38
Stirling, Lt. Col. William, 38
Submarines, midget, 133–5
Sukarno, President, 127–8

Summers, Cpl., 63, 71
Summers, Sgt. 'Safari', 71
Sutherland, David, 19, 26, 30, 31,
    32, 45–7, 54–5, 57, 83, 84,
    99, 101, 105
Syria, 25

T

Talisman, 15
Thomason, Lt., 102
Tilos, 70–1, 75
Tirpitz, 134
Tito, Marshal, 89, 90, 105
Tobruk, 32–6
Tod, Brig., 106–7
Torbay, 15, 19, 21
Traveller, 32
Traveller's Life, A, 19
Tripoli, 20
Triton, 27
Truant, 14
Tuckey, Sub-Lt., 77
Tuna, 130
Turkey, 68

V

Vathi Bay, attack on, 85
Verney, Cpt. J., 61, 62–3
Vikings, 4

Volos, 99
Von Klemann, Gen., 67

W

Watler, Pvt., 36, 55–6
Wavell, Field Marshal Sir
    Archibald, 13, 23, 34–5
Wilson, Lt., 11, 12, 14–15, 19–20,
    35
Wolfe, Gen., 3
Wolseley, Col. Garnet, 2
Woodhouse, Col. C. M., 95

X

X-craft, 114, 123, 134, 135

Y

Yedi, Atala, 70
Yugoslavia, 9, 42, 87, 88
    strategic value of, 89

Z

Zara, 107
Zeebrugge, 112
    raid on, 11
Z Group, 112

THE MEN WHO HOLD THE WORLD'S FUTURE IN THEIR HANDS

THE NUCLEAR BARONS

Peter Pringle and James Spigelman

This superbly researched and forcefully argued account tells for the first time the full story of the nuclear era and its architects. It details the tests and exposes the deadly accidents, cynical cover-ups, ruthless profiteering, megalomanic ignorance and wilful evasions of democratic control which characterise the nuclear industry.

Peter Pringle, a correspondent for the Sunday Times Insight Team and James Spigelman, who held several high-level posts in the Australian Government, have used a worldwide network of sources to trace the devastating tale of nuclear build-up which has led to today's situation.

'There is no shortage of books on all things nuclear, but if you want to read just one . . . this is the book to read.'
New Statesman

WORLD AFFAIRS   0 7221 7029 7   £3.50